Choose Your

A Disciplined Agile Approach
to Optimizing Your Way of Working

Second Edition

Scott W. Ambler

Mark Lines

Library of Congress Cataloging-in-Publication Data has been applied for.

Names: Ambler, Scott W., 1966- author. | Lines, Mark, 1964- author.
Title: Choose your wow! : a disciplined agile approach to optimizing your way of working / Scott W. Ambler, Mark Lines.
Description: Second edition. | Newtown Square, Pennsylvania : Project Management Institute, Inc., [2022] | Includes bibliographical references and index. | Summary: "Hundreds of organizations around the world have already benefited from Disciplined Agile Delivery (DAD). Disciplined Agile® (DA) is the only comprehensive tool kit available for guidance on building high-performance agile teams and optimizing your way of working (WoW). As a hybrid of the leading agile, lean, and traditional approaches, DA provides hundreds of strategies to help you make better decisions within your agile teams, balancing self-organization with the realities and constraints of your unique enterprise context"-- Provided by publisher.
Identifiers: LCCN 2021062503 (print) | LCCN 2021062504 (ebook) | ISBN 9781628257540 (paperback) | ISBN 9781628257557 (ebook)
Subjects: LCSH: Agile software development. | Project management. | Teams in the workplace.
Classification: LCC QA76.76.D47 A42525 2022 (print) | LCC QA76.76.D47 (ebook) | DDC 005.1/112--dc23
LC record available at https://lccn.loc.gov/2021062503
LC ebook record available at https://lccn.loc.gov/2021062504

ISBN: 978-1-62825-754-0

Published by: Project Management Institute, Inc.
                   14 Campus Boulevard
                   Newtown Square, Pennsylvania 19073-3299 USA
                   Phone: +1 610 356 4600
                   Fax: +1 610 356 4647
                   Email: customercare@pmi.org
                   Internet: www.PMI.org

To place a Trade Order or for pricing information, please contact Independent Publishers Group:

          Independent Publishers Group
          Order Department
          814 North Franklin Street
          Chicago, IL 60610 USA
          Phone: 800 888 4741
          Fax: +1 312 337 5985
          Email: orders@ipgbook.com (For orders only)

For all other inquiries, please contact the PMI Book Service Center.

          PMI Book Service Center
          P.O. Box 932683, Atlanta, GA 31193-2683 USA
          Phone: 866 276 4764 (within the U.S. or Canada) or +1 770 280 4129 (globally)
          Fax: +1 770 280 4113
          Email: info@bookorders.pmi.org

Foreword

All models are wrong, but some are useful.
—George Box, 1978

You are special; you are a beautiful and unique snowflake. So are your family, your friends, your communities, your team, your peers, your colleagues, your business area, your organization. No other organization has the same collections of people, the same behavioral norms, the same processes, the same current state, the same impediments, the same customers, the same brand, the same values, the same history, the same folklore, the same identity, the same "this is the way we do things round here" as yours does.

Your organization's behavior is emergent. The whole is greater than the sum of the parts, the whole has unique properties that the individuals don't have. Acting in the space, changes the space. Individual and collective behaviors mutate and self-organize on a change-initiating event. Interventions are irreversible, like adding milk to coffee. The system changes. People don't forget what happened and what the outcome was. The system learns. Next time, the response to the change event will be different, either for the better or for the worse, reflecting what happened last time and based on incentivization. Not only are your contexts unique, they are constantly changing and changing how they change.

With this uniqueness, emergence, and adaptation, it is not possible to have one set of practices which will optimize outcomes for every context. One set of practices might improve outcomes for one context at one point in time. Over time, as the system changes with new impediments and new enablers, it will no longer be optimal. One size does not fit all. There is no snake oil to cure all ills. Your organization has tens, hundreds, or thousands of contexts within contexts, each one unique. Applying one size fits all across many contexts may raise some boats; however, it will sink other boats and hold back many more boats from rising.

How practices are adopted is also important, not only what the practices are. For lasting improvement and to apply an agile mindset to agility, the locus of control needs to be internal. People need to have autonomy and empowerment within guardrails to be able to experiment in order to improve on desired outcomes. High alignment and high autonomy are both needed. Not an imposition top down, which is disempowering, with the locus of control being external. With imposition, people will not take responsibility for what happens, and will knowingly do things which are detrimental, a behavior known as agentic state.

Disciplined Agile® (DA™) is designed to cater to these realities, the characteristics of uniqueness, emergence, and adaption. Disciplined Agile provides guardrails, guidance, and enterprise awareness. It is unique in this regard. It provides a common vocabulary, minimal viable guardrails, which in turn enables empowerment and autonomy for teams and teams of teams to improve on their outcomes how they see fit, with an internal locus of control. Not everyone should follow a mandated, synchronized, iteration-based approach, for example. In my experience, in a large organization with more than one context, synchronized iterations suit one context (e.g., many teams on one product with a low level of mastery and with dependencies which have not been removed or alleviated) and do not suit 99 other contexts. It is not applying an agile mindset to agility. Some business areas are better off adopting a Kanban approach from the beginning, especially if there is a pathological culture where messengers are shot. Evolution over revolution stands a chance of progress. Revolution will struggle; with a lack of psychological safety, the antibodies will be strong. Some business areas, with people who have been working this way in islands of agility for more than 20 years and with psychological safety, may choose to take a more revolutionary approach, as the soil is more fertile, people are more willing, and failed experiments are viewed positively.

Disciplined Agile enables a heterogeneous, not homogeneous, approach across diverse, complex organizations. It includes principles of "choice is good," "context counts," and "enterprise awareness." It enables the discipline that organizations need, while not forcing round pegs into square holes. It provides a common vocabulary and, with the process goals, it provides options to consider in your unique context with varying levels of mastery. This requires people to think rather than follow orders, to take ownership and experiment to achieve specific outcomes, not pursue agile for agile's sake. This is harder than following a prescription or a *diktat*, it requires servant leadership and coaching, in the same way as learning to drive, ski, play a musical instrument, or play in an orchestra or a team sport. As one size does not fit all, as there is no prescription (for example, it is a fallacy to copy "the Spotify Model" firm-wide, which even Spotify® says is not the Spotify Model), this context-sensitive, invitation-over-imposition approach leads to better outcomes and is more likely to stick, as it has come from within, the locus of control is internal, and it is owned. There is no one else to blame and no one artificially keeping the elastic band stretched. It starts to build a muscle of continuous improvement.

Within Disciplined Agile, if teams choose to adopt Scrum; a Scrum-scaled pattern such as LeSS, SAFe®, Nexus®, or Scrum at Scale; or adopt an evolutionary pull-based, limited work-in-progress approach, with a view that it will optimize outcomes in their unique context, they are free to do so: #allframeworks, not #noframeworks or #oneframework. Across an organization, DA provides the minimal viable commonality as well as guidance, which is needed for anything other than the simplest of firms.

The job you are hiring Disciplined Agile to do is to enable context-sensitive, heterogeneous approaches to agility, which will maximize outcomes organization-wide. As with everything, treat it as a departure point, not a destination. As your organization-wide level of mastery increases, keep on inspecting and adapting. This book is an indispensable guide for those looking to optimize ways of working in heterogeneous organizations.

Jonathan Smart @jonsmart
Enterprise Agility Lead, Deloitte
Former Head of Ways of Working, Barclays

Preface

Software development is incredibly straightforward, and if we may be so bold, it is very likely the simplest endeavor in modern organizations. It requires very little technical skill at all, requires little to no collaboration on the part of developers, and is so mundane and repetitive that anyone can create software by following a simple, repeatable process. The handful of software development techniques were established and agreed to decades ago, are easily learned in only a few days, and are both well accepted and well known by all software practitioners. Our stakeholders can clearly communicate their needs early in the life cycle, are readily available and eager to work with us, and never change their minds. The software and data sources created in the past are high quality, easy to understand and to evolve, and come with fully automated regression test suites and high-quality supporting documentation. Software development teams always have complete control of their destiny, and are supported by effective corporate governance, procurement, and financing practices that reflect and enable the realities we face. And, of course, it is easy to hire and retain talented software developers.

Sadly, very little if anything in the previous paragraph is even remotely similar to the situation faced by your organization today. Software development is complex, the environments in which software developers work is complex, the technologies that we work with are complex and constantly changing, and the problems that we are asked to solve are complex and evolving. It is time to embrace this complexity, to accept the situation that we face, and to choose to deal with it head on.

Why You Need to Read This Book

One of the agile principles is that a team should regularly reflect and strive to improve their strategy. One way to do that is the sailboat retrospective game, where we ask what are the anchors holding us back, what rocks or storms should we watch out for, and what is the wind in our sails that will propel us to success. So let's play this game for the current state of agile product development in the context of someone, presumably you, who is hoping to help their team choose and evolve their way of working (WoW).

First, there are several things that are potentially holding us back:

1. **Product development is complex.** As professionals, we get paid a lot of money because what we do is complex. Our WoW must address how to approach requirements, architecture, testing, design, programming, management, deployment, governance, and many other aspects of software/product development in a myriad of ways. And it must describe how to do this throughout the entire life cycle from beginning to end, and also address the unique situation that our team faces. In many ways, this book holds up a mirror to the complexities faced by software developers and provides a flexible, context-sensitive tool kit to deal with it.
2. **Agile industrial complex (AIC).** Martin Fowler, in a conference keynote in Melbourne in August 2018, coined the phrase "agile industrial complex" [Fowler]. He argued that we are now in the era of the AIC, with prescriptive frameworks being routinely imposed upon teams as well as upon the entire organization, presumably to provide management with a modicum of control over this crazy agile stuff. In such environments, a set of processes defined by the chosen framework

will now be "deployed"—whether it makes sense for your team or not. We are deploying this, you will like it, you will own it—but don't dream of trying to change or improve it because management is hoping to "limit the variability of team processes." As Cynefin advises, you can't solve a complex problem by applying a simple solution [Cynefin].

3. **Agile growth greatly exceeded the supply of experienced coaches.** Although there are some great agile coaches out there, unfortunately their numbers are insufficient to address the demand. Effective coaches have great people skills and years of experience, not days of training, in the topic that they are coaching you in. In many organizations, we find coaches who are effectively learning on the job, in many ways similar to college professors who are reading one chapter ahead of their students. They can address the straightforward problems but struggle with anything too far beyond what the AIC processes inflicted upon them deign to address.

There are also several things to watch out for that could cause us to run aground:

- **False promises.** You may have heard agile coaches claim to achieve 10 times productivity increases through adoption of agile, yet are unable to provide any metrics to back up these claims. Or perhaps you've read a book that claims in its title that Scrum enables you to do twice the work in half the time [Sutherland]? Yet the reality is that organizations are seeing, on average, closer to 7–12% improvements on small teams and 3–5% improvements on teams working at scale [Reifer].

- **More silver bullets.** How do you kill a werewolf? A single shot with a silver bullet. In the mid-1980s, Fred Brooks taught us that there is no single change that you can make in the software development space, no technology that you can buy, no process you can adopt, no tool you can install, that will give you the order of magnitude productivity improvement that you're likely hoping for [Brooks]. In other words, there's no silver bullet for software development, regardless of the promises of the schemes where you become a "certified master" after 2 days of training, a program consultant after 4 days of training, or any other quick-fix promises. What you do need are skilled, knowledgeable, and hopefully experienced people working together effectively.

- **Process populism.** We often run into organizations where leadership's decision-making process when it comes to software process boils down to "ask an industry analyst firm what's popular" or "what are my competitors adopting?" rather than what is the best fit for our situation. Process populism is fed by false promises and leadership's hope to find a silver bullet to the very significant challenges that they face around improving their organization's processes. Most agile methods and frameworks are prescriptive, regardless of their marketing claims—when you're given a handful of techniques out of the thousands that exist, and not given explicit options for tailoring those techniques, that's pretty much as prescriptive as it gets. We appreciate that many people just want to be told what to do, but unless that method/framework actually addresses the real problem that you face, then adopting it likely isn't going to do much to help the situation.

Luckily, there are several things that are the "winds in our sails" that propel you to read this book:

- **It embraces your uniqueness.** This book recognizes that your team is unique and faces a unique situation. No more false promises of a "one-size-fits-all" process that requires significant, and risky, disruption to adopt.

- **It embraces the complexity you face.** Disciplined Agile® (DA™) effectively holds up a mirror to the inherent complexities that you face, and presents an accessible representation to help guide your process improvement efforts. No more simplistic, silver bullet methods or process frameworks that gloss over the myriad of challenges your organizations faces, because to do so wouldn't fit in well with the certification training they're hoping to sell you.

- **It provides explicit choices.** This book provides the tools you need to make better process decisions that in turn will lead to better outcomes. In short, it enables your team to own their own process, to choose their way of working (WoW) that reflects the overall direction of your organization. This book presents a proven strategy for guided continuous improvement (GCI), a team-based process improvement strategy, rather than naïve adoption of a "populist process."
- **It provides agnostic advice.** This book isn't limited to the advice of a single framework or method, nor is it limited to agile and lean. Our philosophy is to look for great ideas regardless of their source and to recognize that there are no best practices (nor worst practices). When we learn a new technique, we strive to understand what its strengths and weaknesses are and in what situations to (not) apply it.

In our training, we often get comments like "I wish I knew this 5 years ago," "I wish my Scrum coaches knew this now," or "Going into this workshop I thought I knew everything about agile development, boy was I wrong." We suspect you're going to feel the exact same way about this book.

How This Book Is Organized

This book is organized into seven chapters:

- **Chapter 1: Choosing Your WoW!** An overview of the Disciplined Agile (DA) tool kit.
- **Chapter 2: Being Disciplined.** The values, principles, and philosophies for disciplined agilists.
- **Chapter 3: Disciplined Agile Delivery in a Nutshell.** An overview of Disciplined Agile Delivery (DAD), the solution delivery portion of the DA tool kit.
- **Chapter 4: Roles, Rights, and Responsibilities.** A discussion of individuals and interactions.
- **Chapter 5: The Process Goals.** How to focus on process outcomes rather than conform to process prescriptions so that your team has a fit-for-purpose approach.
- **Chapter 6: Choosing the Right Life Cycle.** How teams can work in unique ways, yet still be governed consistently.
- **Chapter 7: Disciplined Success.** Where to go from here.

And of course, there is the back matter, including references, a list of abbreviations, and an index.

Who This Book Is For

This book is for people who want to improve their team's way of working (WoW). It's for people who are willing to think outside of the "agile box" and experiment with new WoWs, regardless of their agile purity. It's for people who realize that context counts, that everyone faces a unique situation and will work in their own unique way, and that one process does not fit all. It's for people who realize that, although they are in a unique situation, others have faced similar situations before and have figured out a variety of strategies that you can adopt and tailor—you can reuse the process learnings of others and thereby invest your energies into adding critical business value to your organization.

Our aim in writing this book is to provide an overview of DA with a focus on the DAD portion of it.

Acknowledgments

We would like to thank the following individuals for all of their input and the hard work they invested to help us write this book. We couldn't have done it without you.

Beverley Ambler
Joshua Barnes
Klaus Boedker
Kiron Bondale
Tom Boulet
Paul Carvalho
Chris Celsie
Daniel Gagnon
Drennan Govender
Bjorn Gustafsson
Michelle Harrison
Michael Kogan
Katherine Lines
Louise Lines
Glen Little
Lana Miles
Valentin Tudor Mocanu
Maciej Mordaka
Charlie Mott
Jerry Nicholas
Edson Portilho
Simon Powers
Aldo Rall
Frank Schophuizen
Al Shalloway
David Shapiro
Paul Sims
Kim Shinners
Jonathan Smart
Roly Stimson
Jim Trott
Klaas van Gend
Abhishek Vernal
Jaco Viljoen

Contents

Chapter 1

Choosing Your WoW!

A man's pride can be his downfall, and he needs to learn when to turn to others for support and guidance. —Bear Grylls

---

Key Points in This Chapter

- Disciplined Agile Delivery (DAD) teams have the autonomy to choose their way of working (WoW).
- You need to both "be agile" and know how to "do agile."
- Software development is complicated; there's no easy answer for how to do it.
- Disciplined Agile® (DA™) provides the scaffolding—a tool kit of agnostic advice—to Choose Your WoW™.
- Other people have faced, and overcome, similar challenges to yours. DA enables you to leverage their learnings.
- You can use this book to guide how to initially choose your WoW and then evolve it over time.
- The real goal is to effectively achieve desired organizational outcomes, not to be/do agile.
- Better decisions lead to better outcomes.

Welcome to *Choose Your WoW*, the book about how agile software development teams, or more accurately agile/lean solution delivery teams, can choose their WoW. This chapter describes some fundamental concepts around why choosing your WoW is important, fundamental strategies for how to do so, and how this book can help you to become effective at it.

Why Should Teams Choose Their WoW?

Agile teams are commonly told to own their process, to choose their WoW. This is very good advice for several reasons:

- **Context counts.** People and teams will work differently depending on the context of their situation. Every person is unique, every team is unique, and every team finds itself in a unique situation. A team of five people will work differently than a team of 20, than a team of 50. A team in a life-critical regulatory situation will work differently than a team in a nonregulatory situation. Our team will work differently than your team because we're different people with our own unique skill sets, preferences, and backgrounds.

- **Choice is good.** To be effective, a team must be able to choose the practices and strategies to address the situation that they face. The implication is that they need to know what these choices are, what the trade-offs are of each, and when (or when not) to apply each one. In other words, they either need to have a deep background in software process, something that few people have, or have a good guide to help them make these process-related choices. Luckily, this book is a very good guide.
- **We should optimize flow.** We want to be effective in the way that we work, and ideally to delight our customers/stakeholders in doing so. To do this, we need to optimize the workflow within our team and in how we collaborate with other teams across the organization.
- **We want to be awesome.** Who wouldn't want to be awesome at what they do? Who wouldn't want to work on an awesome team or for an awesome organization? A significant part of being awesome is to enable teams to choose their WoW and to allow them to constantly experiment to identify even better ways they can work.

In short, we believe that it's time to take back agile. Martin Fowler recently coined the term "agile industrial complex" to refer to the observation that many teams are following a "faux agile" strategy, sometimes called "agile in name only" (AINO). This is often the result of organizations adopting a prescriptive framework, such as the Scaled Agile Framework (SAFe®) [SAFe], and then forcing teams to adopt it regardless of whether it actually makes sense to do so (and it rarely does), or forcing teams to follow an organizational standard application of Scrum [ScrumGuide; SchwaberBeedle]. Yet canonical agile is very clear; it's individuals and interactions over processes and tools—teams should be allowed, and better yet, supported, to choose and then evolve their WoW.

You Need to "Be Agile" *and* Know How to "Do Agile"

Scott's daughter, Olivia, is 11 years old. She and her friends are some of the most agile people we've ever met. They're respectful (as much as 11-year-old children can be), they're open-minded, they're collaborative, they're eager to learn, and they're always experimenting. They clearly embrace an agile mindset, yet if we were to ask them to develop software it would be a disaster. Why? Because they don't have the skills. Similarly, it would be a disaster to ask them to negotiate a multimillion-dollar contract, to develop a marketing strategy for a new product, to lead a 4,000-person value stream, and so on. They could gain these skills in time, but right now they just don't know what they're doing even though they are very agile. We've also seen teams made up of millennials who collaborate very naturally and have the skills to perform their jobs, although perhaps are not yet sufficiently experienced to understand the enterprise-class implications of their work. And, of course, we've seen teams of people with decades of experience but very little experience doing so collaboratively. None of these situations are ideal. Our point is that it's absolutely critical to have an agile mindset, to "be agile," but you also need to have the requisite skills to "do agile" and the experience to "do enterprise agile." An important aspect of this book is that it comprehensively addresses the potential skills required by agile/lean teams to succeed.

The real goal is to effectively achieve desired organizational outcomes, not to be/do agile. What good is it to be working in an agile manner if you're producing the wrong thing, or producing something you already have, or are producing something that doesn't fit into the overall direction of your organization? Our real focus must be on achieving the outcomes that will make our organization successful, and becoming more effective in our WoW will help us to do that.

Accept That There's No Easy Answer

What we do as professionals is challenging, otherwise we would have been automated out of jobs by now. You and your team work within the context of your organization, using a collection of technologies that are evolving, and for a wide variety of business needs. And you're working with people with different backgrounds, different preferences, different experiences, different career goals, and they may report to a different group or even a different organization than you do.

We believe in embracing this complexity because it's the only way to be effective, and better yet, to be awesome. When we downplay or even ignore important aspects of our WoW, say architecture for example, we tend to make painful mistakes in that area. When we denigrate aspects of our WoW, such as governance, perhaps because we've had bad experiences in the past with not-so-agile governance, then we risk people outside of our team taking responsibility for that aspect and inflicting their non-agile practices upon us. In this way, rather than enabling our agility, they act as impediments.

We Can Benefit From the Learnings of Others

A common mistake that teams make is that they believe that just because they face a unique situation, that they need to figure out their WoW from scratch. Nothing could be further from the truth. When you approach and develop a new application, do you develop a new language, a new compiler, new code libraries, and so on, from scratch? Of course not, you adopt the existing things that are out there, combine them in a unique way, and then modify them as needed. Development teams, regardless of technology, utilize proven frameworks and libraries to improve productivity and quality. It should be the same thing with process. As you can see in this book, there are hundreds, if not thousands, of practices and strategies out there that have been proven in practice by thousands of teams before you. You don't need to start from scratch, but instead can develop your WoW by combining existing practices and strategies and then modifying them appropriately to address the situation at hand. DA provides the tool kit to guide you through this in a streamlined and accessible manner. Since our first book on DAD [AmblerLines2012], we have received feedback that while it is seen as an extremely rich collection of strategies and practices, practitioners sometimes struggle to understand how to reference the strategies and apply them. One of the goals of this book is to make DAD more accessible so that you can easily find what you need to customize your WoW.

One thing that you'll notice throughout the book is that we provide a lot of references. We do this for three reasons: First, to give credit where credit is due. Second, to let you know where you can go for further details. Third, to enable us to focus on summarizing the various ideas and to put them into context, rather than going into the details of every single one. Our approach to references is to use the format: [MeaningfulName], where there is a corresponding entry in the references at the back of the book.

DA Knowledge Makes You a Far More Valuable Team Member

We have heard from many organizations using DA—and they permit us to quote them—that team members who have invested in learning DA (and proving it through challenging certifications) become more valuable contributors. The reason, to us, is quite clear. Understanding a larger library

of proven strategies means that teams will make better decisions and "fail fast" less, and rather "learn and succeed earlier." A lack of collective self-awareness of the available options is a common source of teams struggling to meet their agility expectations—and that is exactly what happens when you adopt prescriptive methods/frameworks that don't provide you with choices. Every team member, especially consultants, is expected to bring a tool kit of ideas to customize the team's process as part of self-organization. A larger tool kit and commonly understood terminology is a good thing.

The Disciplined Agile (DA) Tool Kit Provides Accessible Guidance

One thing that we have learned over time is that some people, while they understand the concepts of DA by either reading the books or attending a workshop, struggle with how to apply DA. DA is an extremely rich body of knowledge that is presented in an accessible manner.

The good news is that the content of this book is organized by the goals, and that by using the goal-driven approach, it is easy to find the guidance that you need for the situation at hand. Here's how you can apply this tool kit in your daily work to be more effective in achieving your desired outcomes:

- Contextualized process reference
- Guided continuous improvement (GCI)
- Process-tailoring workshops
- Enhanced retrospectives
- Enhanced coaching

Contextualized Process Reference

As we described earlier, this book is meant to be a reference. You will find it handy to keep this book nearby to quickly reference available strategies when you face particular challenges. This book presents you with process choices and, more importantly, puts those choices into context. DA provides three levels of scaffolding to do this:

1. **Life cycles.** At the highest level of WoW guidance are life cycles, the closest that DAD gets to methodology. DAD supports six different life cycles, as you can see in Figure 1.1, to provide teams with the flexibility of choosing an approach that makes the most sense for them. Chapter 6 explores the life cycles, and how to choose between them, in greater detail. It also describes how teams can still be governed consistently even though they're working in different ways.

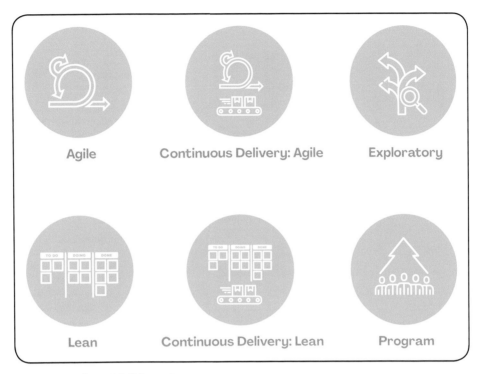

Figure 1.1 The DAD life cycles.

2. **Process goals.** Figure 1.2 presents the goal diagram for the Improve Quality process goal, and Figure 1.3 overviews the notation of goal diagrams. DAD is described as a collection of 24 process goals, or process outcomes, if you like. Each goal is described as a collection of decision points, issues that your team needs to determine whether they need to address, and if so, how they will do so. Potential practices/strategies for addressing a decision point, which can be combined in many cases, are presented as lists. Goal diagrams are similar conceptually to mind maps, albeit with the extension of the arrow to represent relative effectiveness of options in some cases. Goal diagrams are, in effect, straightforward guides to help a team to choose the best strategies that they are capable of performing right now given their skills, culture, and situation. Chapter 5 explores the goal-driven approach in greater detail.

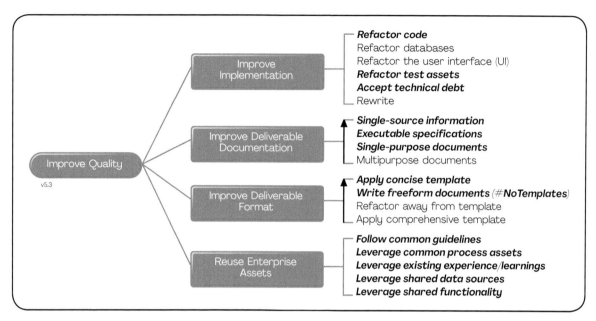

Figure 1.2 The Improve Quality process goal.

3. **Practices/strategies.** At the most granular level of WoW guidance are practices and strategies, depicted on goal diagrams in the lists on the right-hand side. An important implication of goal diagrams, such as the one in Figure 1.2, is that you need less process expertise to identify potential practices/strategies to try out. What you do need is an understanding of the fundamentals of DA, described in this book, and familiarity with the goal diagrams so that you can quickly locate potential options. You do not need to memorize all of your available options because you can look them up, and you don't need to have deep knowledge of each option because they're overviewed and put into context in the Disciplined Agile Browser [DABrowser]. Figure 1.4 shows such an example. In this case, you can see some of the information describing the Improve Implementation decision points of the Improve Quality process goal. You can see a description of the decision point plus the first two options (in the tool you would scroll down for the rest of the options).

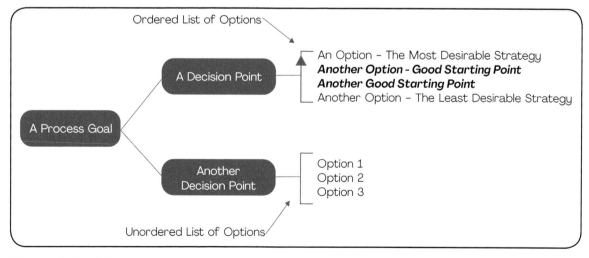

Figure 1.3 Goal diagram notation.

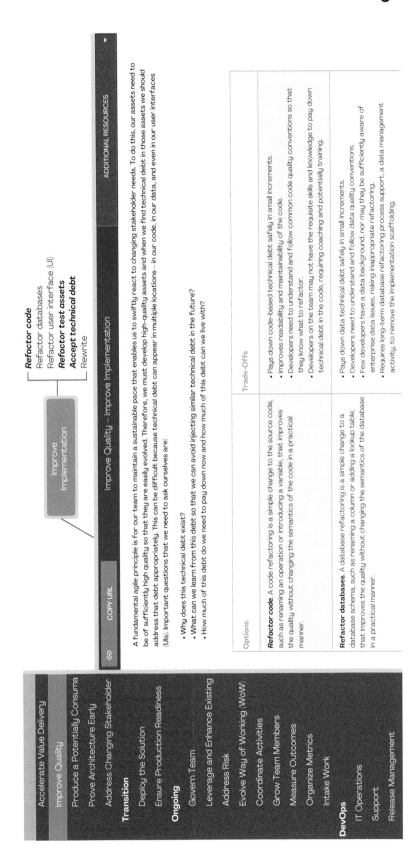

Figure 1.4 Technique details captured in the DA Browser.

Improvement Occurs at Many Levels

Process improvement, or WoW evolution, occurs across your organization. Organizations are a collection of interacting teams and groups, each of which evolves continuously. As teams evolve their WoWs, they motivate changes in the teams they interact with. Because of this constant process evolution, hopefully for the better, and because people are unique, it becomes unpredictable how people are going to work together or what the results of that work will be. In short, your organization is a complex adaptive system (CAS) [Cynefin]. This concept is overviewed in Figure 1.5, which depicts teams, organization areas (such as divisions, lines of business, or value streams), and enterprise teams. Figure 1.5 is a simplification because the diagram is complicated enough as it is—there are far more interactions between teams and across organizational boundaries, and in large enterprises, an organizational area may have its own "enterprise" groups, such as enterprise architecture or finance.

There are several interesting implications for choosing your WoW:

1. **Every team will have a different WoW.** We really can't say this enough.
2. **We will evolve our WoW to reflect learnings whenever we work with other teams.** Not only do we accomplish whatever outcome we set to achieve by working with another team, we very often learn new techniques from them or new ways of collaborating with them (that they may have picked up from working with other teams).
3. **We can purposefully choose to learn from other teams.** There are many strategies that we can choose to adopt within our organization to share learnings across teams, including practitioner presentations, communities of practice (CoPs)/guilds, coaching, and many others. Team-level

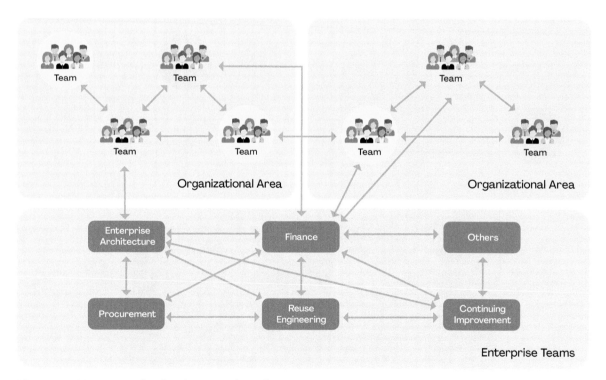

Figure 1.5 Your organization is a complex adaptive system (CAS).

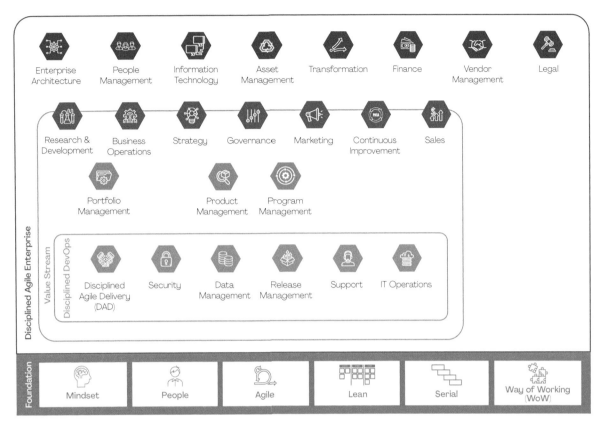

Figure 1.6 The scope of Disciplined Agile.

strategies are captured in the Evolve WoW process goal and organizational-level strategies in the Continuous Improvement process blade[1] [ContinuousImprovement]. In short, the DA tool kit is a generative resource that you can apply in agnostically choosing your WoW.

4. **We can benefit from organizational transformation/improvement efforts.** Improvement can, and should, happen at the team level. It can also happen at the organizational-area level (e.g., we can work to optimize flow between the teams within an area). Improvement also needs to occur outside of DAD teams (e.g., we can help the enterprise architecture, finance, and people management groups to collaborate with the rest of the organization more effectively).

As Figure 1.6 depicts, the DA tool kit is organized into four layers:

1. **Foundation.** The foundation layer provides the conceptual underpinnings of the DA tool kit.
2. **Disciplined DevOps.** DevOps is the streamlining of solution development and operations, and Disciplined DevOps is an enterprise-class approach to DevOps. This layer includes Disciplined Agile Delivery (DAD), the focus of this book, plus other enterprise aspects of DevOps.

---

[1] A process blade addresses a cohesive process area such as asset management, finance, or security.

3. **Value Stream.** The value stream layer is based on Al Shalloway's FLEX, now called DA FLEX. It's not enough to be innovative in ideas if these ideas can't be realized in the marketplace or in the company. DA FLEX is the glue that ties an organization's strategies in that it visualizes what an effective value stream looks like, enabling you to make decisions for improving each part of the organization within the context of the whole.
4. **Disciplined Agile Enterprise (DAE).** The DAE layer focuses on the rest of the enterprise activities that support your organization's value streams.

Teams, regardless of what level they operate at, can and should choose their WoW. Our focus in this book is on DAD teams, although at times we will delve into cross-team and organizational issues where appropriate.

Guided Continuous Improvement (GCI)

Many teams start their agile journey by adopting agile methods such as Scrum [ScrumGuide; SchwaberBeedle], Extreme Programming (XP) [Beck], or Dynamic Systems Development Method (DSDM)-Atern [DSDM]. Large teams dealing with "scale" (we'll discuss what scaling really means in Chapter 2) may choose to adopt SAFe® [SAFe], LeSS [LeSS], or Nexus® [Nexus] to name a few. These methods/frameworks each address a specific class of problem(s) that agile teams face, and from our point of view, they're rather prescriptive in that they don't provide you with many choices. Sometimes, particularly when frameworks are applied to contexts where they aren't an ideal fit, teams often find that they need to invest significant time "descaling" them to remove techniques that don't apply to their situation, then add back in other techniques that do. Having said that, when frameworks are applied in the appropriate context, they can work quite well in practice. When you successfully adopt one of these prescriptive methods/frameworks, your team effectiveness tends to follow the curve shown in Figure 1.7. At first, there is a drop in effectiveness because the team is learning a new way of working, it's investing time in training, and people are often learning new techniques. In time, effectiveness rises, going above what it originally was, but eventually plateaus as the team falls into its new WoW. Things have gotten better, but without concerted effort to improve, you discover that team effectiveness plateaus.

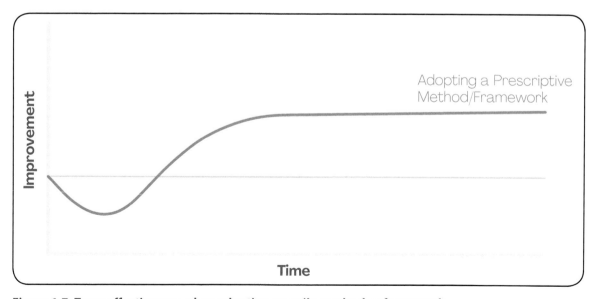

Figure 1.7 Team effectiveness when adopting an agile method or framework.

Some of the feedback that we get about Figure 1.7 is that this can't be, that Scrum promises that you can do twice the work in half the time [Sutherland]. Sadly, this claim of 4 times productivity improvement doesn't seem to hold water in practice. A recent study covering 155 organizations, 1,500 waterfall teams, and 1,500 agile teams found actual productivity increases of agile teams, mostly following Scrum, to be closer to 7–12% [Reifer]. At scale, where the majority of organizations have adopted SAFe, the improvement goes down to 3–5%.

There are many ways that a team can adopt to help them improve their WoW, strategies that are captured by the Evolve WoW process goal. Many people recommend an experimental approach to improvement, and we've found guided experiments to be even more effective. The agile community provides lots of advice around retrospectives, which are working sessions where a team reflects on how they get better, and the lean community gives great advice for how to act on the reflections [Kerth]. Figure 1.8 summarizes W. Edward Deming's plan-do-study-act (PDSA) improvement loop [Deming], sometimes called a kaizen loop. This was Deming's first approach to continuous improvement, which he later evolved to plan-do-check-act (PDCA), which became popular within the business community in the 1990s and the agile community in the early 2000s. But what many people don't know is that after experimenting with PDCA for several years, Deming realized that it wasn't as effective as PDSA and went back to it. The primary difference being that the "study" activity motivated people to measure and think more deeply about whether a change worked well for them in practice. So we've decided to respect Deming's wishes and recommend PDSA rather than PDCA, as we found critical thinking such as this results in improvements that stick. Some people gravitate toward U.S. Air Force Colonel John Boyd's OODA (Observe Orient Decide Act) loop to guide their continuous improvement efforts—as always, our advice is to do what works for you [Coram]. Regardless of which improvement loop you adopt, remember that your team can, and perhaps should, run multiple experiments in parallel, particularly when the potential improvements are on different areas of your process and therefore won't affect each other (if they affect each other, it makes it difficult to determine the effectiveness of each experiment).

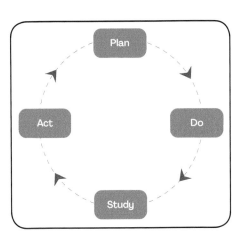

Figure 1.8 The PDSA continuous improvement loop.

The basic idea with the PDSA/PDCA/OODA continuous improvement loop strategy is that you improve your WoW as a series of small changes, a strategy the lean community calls kaizen, which is Japanese for improvement. In Figure 1.9, you see the workflow for running an experiment. The first step is to identify a potential improvement, such as a new practice or strategy, that you want to experiment with to see how well it works for you in the context of your situation. The effectiveness of a potential improvement is determined by measuring against clear outcomes, perhaps identified via a goal question metric (GQM) [GQM] or objectives and key results (OKRs) [Doer]. Measuring the effectiveness of applying the new WoW is an example of validated learning [Ries]. It's important to note that Figure 1.9 provides a detailed description of a single pass through a team's continuous improvement loop.

The value of DA is that it can guide you through this identification step by helping you to agnostically identify a new practice/strategy that is likely to address the challenge you're hoping to address. By doing so, you increase your chance of identifying a potential improvement that works

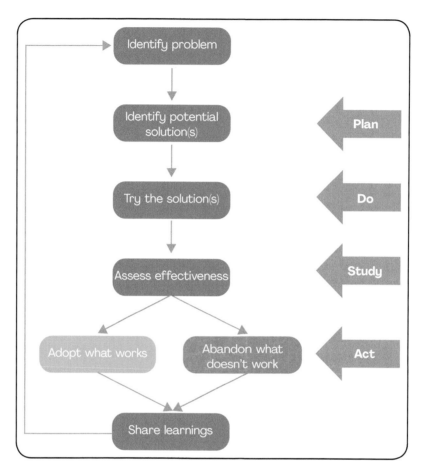

Figure 1.9 An experimental approach to evolving your WoW.

for you, thereby speeding up your efforts to improve your WoW—we call this guided continuous improvement (GCI). In short, at this level, the DA tool kit enables you to become a high-performing team quicker. In the original DAD book, we described a strategy called "measured improvement" that worked in a very similar manner.

A similar strategy that we've found very effective in practice is Lean Change[2] [LeanChange1; LeanChange2], particularly at the organizational level. The Lean Change management cycle, overviewed in Figure 1.10, applies ideas from Lean Startup [Ries] in that you have insights (hypothesis), identify potential options to address your insights, and then run experiments in the form of minimum viable changes (MVCs). These MVCs are introduced, allowed to run for a while, and then the results are measured to determine how effective they are in practice. Teams then can choose to stick with the changes that work well for them in the situation that they face, and abandon changes that don't work well. Where GGI enables teams to become high performing, Lean Change enables high-performing organizations.

---

[2] In DA's Transformation process blade, PMI.org/disciplined-agile/process/transformation, we show how to apply Lean Change at the organizational level.

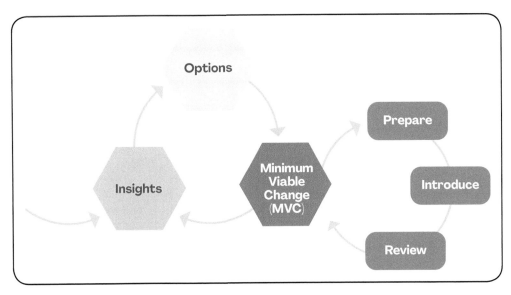

Figure 1.10 The Lean Change management cycle.

The improvement curve for (unguided) continuous improvement strategies is shown in Figure 1.11 as a dashed line. You can see that there is still a bit of a productivity dip at first as teams learn how to identify MVCs and then run the experiments, but this is small and short-lived. The full line depicts the curve for GCI in context; teams are more likely to identify options that will work for them, resulting in a higher rate of positive experiments and thereby a faster rate of improvement. In short, better decisions lead to better outcomes.

Of course, neither of the lines in Figure 1.11 are perfectly smooth. A team will have ups and downs, with some failed experiments (downs) where they learn what doesn't work in their situation, and some successful experiences (ups) where they discover a technique that improves their effectiveness as a team. The full line, representing GCI, will be smoother than the dashed line because teams will have a higher percentage of ups.

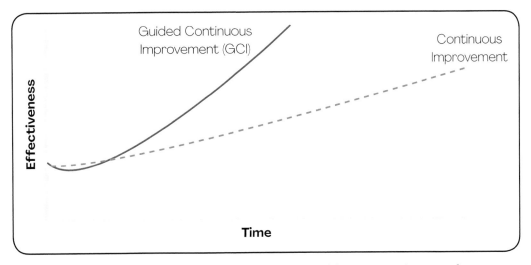

Figure 1.11 Guided continuous improvement (GCI) enables teams to improve faster.

The good news is that these two strategies, adopting a prescriptive method/framework and then improving your WoW through GCI, can be combined, as shown in Figure 1.12. We are constantly running into teams that have adopted a prescriptive agile method, very often Scrum or SAFe, that have plateaued because they've run into one or more issues not directly addressed by their chosen framework/method. Because the method doesn't address the problem(s) they face, and because they don't have expertise in that area, they tend to flounder. Ivar Jacobson has coined the term "they're stuck in method prison" [Prison]. By applying a continuous improvement strategy, or better yet, GCI, their process improvement efforts soon get back on track. Furthermore, because the underlying business situation that you face is constantly shifting, it tells you that you cannot sit on your "process laurels," but instead must adjust your WoW to reflect the evolving situation.

To be clear, GCI at the team level tends to be a simplified version of what you would do at the organizational level. At the team level, teams may choose to maintain an improvement backlog of things they hope to improve. At the organizational area or enterprise levels, we may have a group of people guiding a large transformation or improvement effort that is focused on enabling teams to choose their WoWs and to address larger organizational issues that teams cannot easily address on their own.

Process-Tailoring Workshops

Another common strategy for applying DA to choose your WoW is a process-tailoring workshop [Tailoring]. In a process-tailoring workshop, a coach or team lead walks the team through important

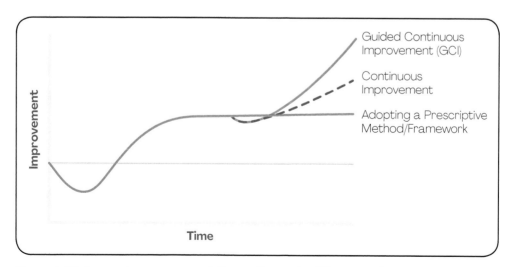

Figure 1.12 Improving upon an existing agile method/framework.

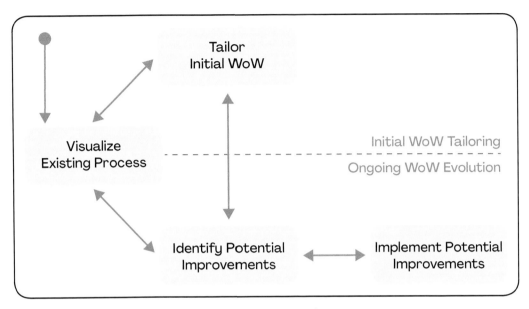

Figure 1.13 Choosing and evolving your WoW over time.

aspects of DAD and the team discusses how they're going to work together. This typically includes choosing a life cycle, walking through the process goals one at a time and addressing the decision points of each one, and discussing roles and responsibilities.

A process-tailoring workshop, or several short workshops, can be run at any time. As shown in Figure 1.13, they are typically performed when a team is initially formed to determine how they will streamline their initiation efforts (what we call the Inception phase), and just before Construction begins to agree on how that effort will be approached. Any process decisions made in process-tailoring workshops are not carved in stone but instead evolve over time as the team learns. You always want to be learning and improving your process as you go, and in fact, most agile teams will regularly reflect on how to do so via holding retrospectives. In short, the purpose of process-tailoring workshops is to get your team going in the right direction, whereas the purpose of retrospectives is to identify potential adjustments to that process.

A valid question to ask is what does the time line look like for evolving the WoW within a team? Jonathan Smart, who guided the transformation at Barclays, recommends Dan North's visualize, stabilize, and optimize time line as depicted in Figure 1.14. You start by visualizing your existing

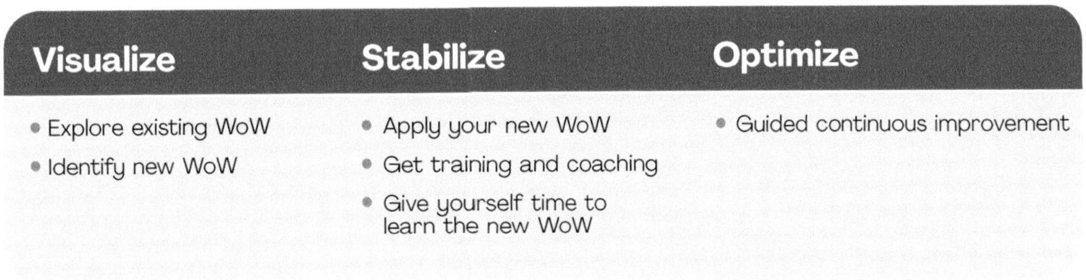

Visualize	Stabilize	Optimize
• Explore existing WoW • Identify new WoW	• Apply your new WoW • Get training and coaching • Give yourself time to learn the new WoW	• Guided continuous improvement

Figure 1.14 A time line for process tailoring and improvement on a team.

Process-Tailoring Workshops in a Large Financial Institution

By Daniel Gagnon

In my experience in running dozens of process-tailoring workshops over several years, with teams of every shape, size, and experience level and in different organizations [Gagnon], interestingly, the most recurring comment is that the workshops "revealed all kinds of options we didn't even realize were options!" Although almost always a bit of a hard sell at the outset, I have yet to work with a team that is unable to quickly grasp and appreciate the value of these activities.

Here are my lessons learned:

1. A team lead, architecture owner, or senior developer can actually stand in for most of the developers in the early stages.
2. Tools help. We developed a simple spreadsheet to capture WoW choices.
3. Teams can make immediate WoW decisions and identify future, more "mature" aspirational choices that they set as improvement goals.
4. We defined a small handful of enterprise-level choices to promote consistency across teams, including some "infrastructure as code" choices.
5. Teams don't have to start from a blank slate, but instead can start with the choices made by a similar team and then tailor it from there.

Here's an important note on determining participation: Ultimately, the teams themselves are the best arbiters of who should attend the sessions at varying stages of advancement. The support will become easier and easier to obtain as the benefits of allowing teams to choose their WoW become apparent.

Daniel Gagnon has coached the adoption of Disciplined Agile in two large Canadian financial institutions and is now a senior agile coach in Quebec.

WoW and then identifying a new potential WoW that the team believes will work for them (this is what the initial tailoring is all about). Then the team needs to apply that new WoW and learn how to make it work in their context. This stabilization phase could take several weeks or months, and once the team has stabilized its WoW it is then in a position to evolve it via a GCI strategy.

The good news is that with effective facilitation, you can keep process-tailoring workshops streamlined. To do this, we suggest that you:

- Schedule several short sessions (you may not need all of them).
- Have a clear agenda (set expectations).
- Invite the entire team (it's their process).
- Have an experienced facilitator (this can get contentious).
- Arrange a flexible work space (this enables collaboration).

A process-tailoring workshop is likely to address several important aspects surrounding our way of working (WoW):

- Determine the rights and responsibilities of team members, which is discussed in detail in Chapter 4.
- How do we intend to organize/structure the team?
- What life cycle will the team follow? See Chapter 6 for more on this.
- What practices/strategies will we follow?
- Do we have a definition of ready (DoR) [Rubin] and, if so, what is it?
- Do we have a definition of done (DoD) [Rubin] and, if so, what is it?
- What tools will we use?

Process-tailoring workshops require an investment in time, but they're an effective way to ensure that team members are well aligned in how they intend to work together. Having said that, you want to keep these workshops as streamlined as possible as they can easily take on a life of their own—the aim is to get going in the right "process direction." You can always evolve your WoW later as you learn what works and what doesn't work for you. Finally, you still need to involve some people who are experienced with agile delivery. DA provides a straightforward tool kit for choosing and evolving your WoW, but you still need the skills and knowledge to apply this tool kit effectively.

While DA provides a library or tool kit of great ideas, in your organization you may wish to apply some limits to the degree of self-organization your teams can apply. In DAD, we recommend self-organization within appropriate governance. As such, what we have seen with organizations that adopt DA is that they sometimes help steer the choices so that teams self-organize within commonly understood organizational "guardrails."

Enhance Retrospectives Through Guided Improvement Options

A retrospective is a technique that teams use to reflect on how effective they are and to hopefully identify potential process improvements to experiment with [Kerth]. As you would guess, DA can be used to help identify improvements that would have a good chance of working for you. As an example, perhaps you are having a discussion regarding excessive requirements churn due to ambiguous user stories and acceptance criteria. The observation may be that you need additional requirements models to clarify the requirements. But which models to choose? Referring to the Explore Scope process goal, you could choose to create a domain diagram to clarify the relationships between entities, or perhaps a low-fidelity user interface (UI) prototype to clarify user experience (UX). We have observed that by using DA as a reference, teams are exposed to strategies and practices that they hadn't even heard of before.

Enhance Coaching by Extending the Coach's Process Tool Kit

DA is particularly valuable for agile coaches. First, an understanding of DA means that you have a larger tool kit of strategies that you can bring to bear to help solve your team's problems. Second, we often see coaches refer to DA to explain that some of the things that the teams or the organization itself sees as "best practices" are actually very poor choices, and that there are better alternatives to consider. Third, coaches use DA to help fill in the gaps in their own experience and knowledge.

Documenting Your WoW

Sigh, we wish we could say that you don't need to document your WoW. But the reality is that you very often do, and for one or more very good reasons:

1. **Regulatory.** Your team works in a regulatory environment where, by law, you need to capture your process—your WoW—somehow.
2. **It's too complicated to remember.** There are a lot of moving parts in your WoW. Consider the goal diagram of Figure 1.2. Your team will choose to adopt several of the strategies called out in it, and that's only one of 24 goals. As we said earlier, solution delivery is complex. We've done our best in DA to reduce this complexity so as to help you to choose your WoW, but we can't remove it completely.
3. **It provides comfort.** Many people are uncomfortable with the idea of not having a "defined process" to follow, particularly when they are new to that process. They like to have something to refer to from time to time to aid their learning. As they become more experienced in the team's WoW, they will refer to the documentation less until finally, they never use it at all.

Because few people like to read process material, we suggest you keep it as straightforward as possible. Follow agile documentation [AgileDocumentation] practices, such as keeping it concise and working closely with the audience (in this case, the team itself) to ensure it meets their actual needs. Here are some options for capturing your WoW:

- Use a simple spreadsheet to capture goal diagram choices.
- Create an A3 (single sheet) overview of the process.
- Put up posters on the wall.
- Capture the process concisely in a wiki.

As we show in the Evolve WoW process goal, there are several strategies that you can choose from to capture your WoW. A common approach is for a team to develop and commit to a working agreement. Working agreements will describe the roles and responsibilities that people will take on the team, the general rights and responsibilities of team members, and very often, the team's process (their WoW). As shown in Figure 1.15, we like to distinguish between two important aspects

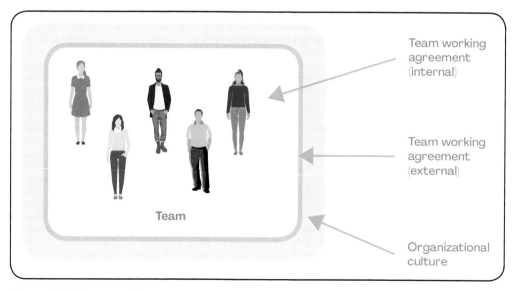

Figure 1.15 Team working agreements.

of a team working agreement—the internal portion of it that describes how the team will work together and the external portion of it that describes how others should interact with the team.

The external portion of a team's working agreement, in some ways, is a service-level agreement (SLA) for the team. It may include a schedule of common meetings that others may attend (for example, daily coordination meetings and upcoming demos), an indication of how to access the team's automated dashboard, how to contact the team, and what the purpose of the team is. The team's working agreement, both the internal and external aspects of it, will, of course, be affected by the organization environment and culture in which it operates.

In Summary

We've worked through several critical concepts in this chapter:

- Disciplined Agile (DA) teams choose their way of working (WoW).
- You need to both "be agile" and know how to "do agile."
- Solution delivery is complicated; there's no easy answer for how to do it.
- DA provides the agnostic scaffolding to support a team in choosing their WoW to deliver software-based solutions.
- Other people have faced, and overcome, similar challenges to yours. DA enables you to leverage their learnings.
- You can use this book to guide how to initially choose your WoW and then evolve it over time.
- A guided continuous improvement (GCI) approach will help your teams to break out of "method prison" and thereby improve their effectiveness.
- The real goal is to effectively achieve desired organizational outcomes, not to be/do agile.
- Better decisions lead to better outcomes.

Chapter 2

Being Disciplined

Better decisions lead to better outcomes.

Key Points in This Chapter

- The Agile Manifesto is a great starting point, but it isn't sufficient.
- Lean principles are critical to success for agile solution delivery teams in the enterprise.
- The DA mindset is based on eight principles, seven promises, and eight guidelines.

What does it mean to be disciplined? To be disciplined is to do the things that we know are good for us, things that usually require hard work and perseverance. It requires discipline to regularly delight our customers. It takes discipline for teams to become awesome. It requires discipline for leaders to ensure that their people have a safe environment to work in. It takes discipline to recognize that we need to tailor our way of working (WoW) for the context that we face, and to evolve our WoW as the situation evolves. It takes discipline to recognize that we are part of a larger organization, that we should do what's best for the enterprise and not just what's convenient for us. It requires discipline to evolve and optimize our overall workflow, and it requires discipline to realize that we have many choices regarding how we work and organize ourselves, so we should choose accordingly.

The Manifesto for Agile Software Development

In 2001, the publication of the *Manifesto for Agile Software Development* [Manifesto], or Agile Manifesto for short, started the agile movement. The manifesto captures four values supported by 12 principles, which are listed below. It was created by a group of 17 people with deep experience in software development. Their goal was to describe what they had found to work in practice rather than describe what they hoped would work in theory. Although it sounds like an obvious thing to do now, back then this was arguably a radical departure from the approach taken by many thought leaders in the software engineering community.

The *Manifesto for Agile Software Development*:
> We are uncovering better ways of developing software by doing it and helping others do it. Through this work, we have come to value:

1. **Individuals and interactions** over processes and tools
2. **Working software** over comprehensive documentation

3. **Customer collaboration** over contract negotiation
4. **Responding to change** over following a plan

That is, while there is value in the items on the right, we value the items on the left more.

There are 12 principles behind the Agile Manifesto that provide further guidance to practitioners. These principles are:

1. Our highest priority is to satisfy the customer through early and continuous delivery of valuable software.
2. Welcome changing requirements, even late in development. Agile processes harness change for the customer's competitive advantage.
3. Deliver working software frequently, from a couple of weeks to a couple of months, with a preference to the shorter timescale.
4. Business people and developers must work together daily throughout the project.
5. Build projects around motivated individuals. Give them the environment and support they need, and trust them to get the job done.
6. The most efficient and effective method of conveying information to and within a development team is face-to-face conversation.
7. Working software is the primary measure of progress.
8. Agile processes promote sustainable development. The sponsors, developers, and users should be able to maintain a constant pace indefinitely.
9. Continuous attention to technical excellence and good design enhances agility.
10. Simplicity—the art of maximizing the amount of work not done—is essential.
11. The best architectures, requirements, and designs emerge from self-organizing teams.
12. At regular intervals, the team reflects on how to become more effective, then tunes and adjusts its behavior accordingly.

The publication of the *Manifesto for Agile Software Development* has proven to be a milestone for the software development world and, as we've seen in recent years, for the business community as well. But time has had its toll, and the manifesto is showing its age in several ways:

1. **It is limited to software development.** The manifesto purposefully focused on software development, not other aspects of IT and certainly not other aspects of our overall enterprise. Many of the concepts can be modified to fit these environments, and they have over the years. Thus, the manifesto provides valuable insights that we can evolve, and it should be evolved and extended for a broader scope than was originally intended.
2. **The software development world has moved on.** The manifesto was crafted to reflect the environment in the 1990s, and some of the principles are out of date. For instance, the third principle suggests that we should deliver software from every few weeks to a couple of months. At the time, it was an accomplishment to have a demonstrable increment of a solution even every month. In modern times, however, the bar is significantly higher, with agile-proficient companies delivering functionality many times a day, in part because the manifesto helped us to get on a better path.
3. **We've learned a lot since then.** Long before agile, organizations were adopting lean ways of thinking and working. Since 2001, agile and lean strategies have not only thrived on their own, but they've been successfully commingled. As we will soon see, this commingling is an inherent

aspect of the DA mindset. DevOps, the merging of software development and IT operations life cycles, has clearly evolved because of this commingling. There are few organizations that haven't adopted, or are at least in the process of adopting, DevOps ways of working—which Chapter 1 showed are an integral part of the DA tool kit. Our point is that it's about more than just agile.

Lean Software Development

The DA mindset is based on a combination of agile and lean thinking. An important starting point for understanding lean thinking is *The Lean Mindset* by Mary and Tom Poppendieck. In this book, they show how the seven principles of lean manufacturing can be applied to optimize the entire value stream. There is great value in this, but we must also remember that most of us are not manufacturing cars—or anything else for that matter. There are several types of work that lean applies to: manufacturing, services, physical-world product development, and (virtual) software development, among others. While we like the groundbreaking work of the Poppendiecks, we prefer to look at the principles to see how they can apply anywhere [Poppendieck]. These principles are:

1. **Eliminate waste.** Lean-thinking advocates regard any activity that does not directly add value to the finished product as waste [WomackJones]. The three biggest sources of waste in our work are the addition of unrequired features, project churn, and crossing organizational boundaries (particularly between stakeholders and development teams). To reduce waste, it is critical that teams be allowed to self-organize and operate in a manner that reflects the work they're trying to accomplish. In product development work (the physical or virtual world), we spend considerable time discovering what is of value. Doing this is not waste. We've seen many folks have endless debates on what waste is because of this. We propose that a critical waste to eliminate is the waste of time due to delays in workflow. On reflection, it can be verified that most waste is reflected, even caused by, delays in workflow. We build unrequired features because we build too-large batches and have delays in feedback as to whether they are needed (or we're not writing our acceptance tests, which delays understanding what we need). Project churn (in particular, errors) is almost always due to getting out of sync without realizing we are. Crossing organizational boundaries is almost always an action that incurs delays as one part of the organization waits for the other.

2. **Build quality in.** Our process should not allow defects to occur in the first place, but when this isn't possible, we should work in such a way that we do a bit of work, validate it, fix any issues that we find, and then iterate. Inspecting after the fact and queuing up defects to be fixed at some time in the future isn't as effective. Agile practices that build quality into our process include test-driven development (TDD) and nonsolo development practices, such as pair programming, mob programming, and modeling with others (mob modeling). All of these techniques are described later in this book.

3. **Create knowledge.** Planning is useful, but learning is essential. We want to promote strategies, such as working iteratively, that help teams discover what stakeholders really want and act on that knowledge. It's also important for team members to regularly reflect on what they're doing and then act to improve their approach through experimentation.

4. **Defer commitment.** It's not necessary to start solution development by defining a complete specification, and in fact that appears to be a questionable strategy at best. We can support the business effectively through flexible architectures that are change-tolerant and by scheduling irreversible decisions for when we have more information and our decisions will be better—the last possible moment. Frequently, deferring commitment until the last responsible moment

requires the ability to closely couple end-to-end business scenarios to capabilities developed in multiple applications by multiple teams. In fact, a strategy of deferring commitments to projects is a way of keeping our options open [Denning]. Software offers some additional mechanisms for deferring commitment. Using emergent design, automated testing, and pattern thinking, essential decisions can often be deferred with virtually no cost. In many ways, agile software development is based on the concept that incremental delivery takes little extra implementation time while enabling developers to save mountains of effort that would otherwise be built on creating features that were not useful.

5. **Deliver quickly.** It is possible to deliver high-quality solutions quickly. By limiting the work of a team to what is within its capacity, we can establish a reliable and repeatable flow of work. An effective organization doesn't demand teams do more than they are capable of, but instead asks them to self-organize and determine what outcomes they can accomplish. Constraining teams to delivering potentially shippable solutions on a regular basis motivates them to stay focused on continuously adding value.

6. **Respect people.** The Poppendiecks also observe that sustainable advantage is gained from engaged, thinking people. The implication is that we need a lean approach to governance, which is the focus of the Govern Team process goal that centers on motivating and enabling teams—not on controlling them.

7. **Optimize the whole.** If we want to be effective at a solution, we must look at the bigger picture. We need to understand the high-level business processes that a value stream supports—processes that often cross multiple systems and multiple teams. We need to manage programs of interrelated efforts so we can deliver a complete product/service to our stakeholders. Measurements should address how well we're delivering business value, and the team should be focused on delivering valuable outcomes to its stakeholders.

The Disciplined Agile Mindset

The Disciplined Agile mindset is summarized in Figure 2.1 and is described as a collection of principles, promises, and guidelines. We like to say that we believe in these eight principles, so we promise to one another that we will work in a disciplined manner and follow a collection of guidelines that enable us to be effective.

We Believe in These Principles

Let's begin with the eight principles behind the Disciplined Agile (DA) tool kit. These ideas aren't new; there is a plethora of sources from which these ideas have emerged, including Alistair Cockburn's work around Heart of Agile [CockburnHeart], Joshua Kerievsky's Modern Agile [Kerievsky], and, of course, the *Agile Manifesto for Software Development* described earlier. In fact, the DA tool kit has always been a hybrid of great strategies from the very beginning, with the focus being on how all of these strategies fit together in practice. While we have a strong belief in a scientific approach and what works, we're agnostic as to how we get there. The DA mindset starts with eight fundamental principles:

- Delight customers
- Be awesome
- Context counts

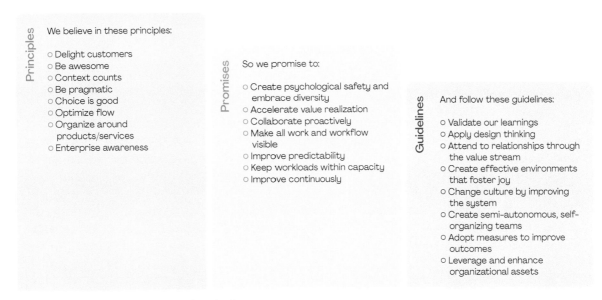

Figure 2.1 The Disciplined Agile mindset.

- Be pragmatic
- Choice is good
- Optimize flow
- Organize around products/services
- Enterprise awareness

Principle: Delight Customers

Customers are delighted when our products and services not only fulfill their needs and expectations, but surpass them. Consider the last time you checked into a hotel. If you're lucky, there was no line, your room was available, and there was nothing wrong with it when you got there. You were likely satisfied with the service, but that's about it. Now imagine that you were greeted by name by the concierge when you arrived, that your favorite snack was waiting for you in the room, and that you received a complimentary upgrade to a room with a magnificent view—all without asking. This would be more than satisfying and would very likely delight you. Although the upgrade won't happen every time you check in, it's a nice touch when it does and you're likely to stick with that hotel chain because they treat you so well.

Successful organizations offer great products and services that delight their customers. Systems design tells us to build with the customer in mind, to work with them closely, and to build in small increments and then seek feedback, so that we better understand what will actually delight them. As disciplined agilists, we embrace change because we know that our stakeholders will see new possibilities as they learn what they truly want as the solution evolves. We also strive to discover what our customers want and to care for our customers. It's much easier to take care of an existing customer than it is to get a new one. Jeff Gothelf and Josh

Seiden say it best in *Sense & Respond:* "If you can make a product easier to use, reduce the time it takes a customer to complete a task, or provide the right information at the exact moment, you win" [SenseRespond].

Principle: Be Awesome

Who doesn't want to be awesome? Who doesn't want to be part of an awesome team doing awesome things while working for an awesome organization? We all want these things. Recently, Joshua Kerievsky has popularized the concept that modern agile teams make people awesome, and, of course, it isn't much of a leap that we want awesome teams and awesome organizations, too. Similarly, Mary and Tom Poppendieck observe that sustainable advantage is gained from engaged, thinking people, as does Richard Sheridan in *Joy Inc.* [Sheridan]. Helping people to be awesome is important because, as Richard Branson of the Virgin Group says, "Take care of your employees and they'll take care of your business."

There are several things that we, as individuals, can do to be awesome. First and foremost, act in such a way that we earn the respect and trust of our colleagues: Be reliable, be honest, be open, be ethical, and treat them with respect. Second, willingly collaborate with others. Share information with them when asked, even if it is a work in progress. Offer help when it's needed and, just as important, reach out for help yourself. Third, be an active learner. We should seek to master our craft, always being on the lookout for opportunities to experiment and learn. Go beyond our specialty and learn about the broader software process and business environment. By becoming a T-skilled, "generalizing specialist," we will be able to better appreciate where others are coming from and thereby interact with them more effectively [Agile Modeling]. Fourth, seek to never let the team down. Yes, it will happen sometimes, and good teams understand and forgive that. Fifth, Simon Powers [Powers] points out that we need to be willing to improve and manage our emotional responses to difficult situations. Innovation requires diversity, and by their very nature, diverse opinions may cause emotional reactions. We must all work on making our workplace psychologically safe.

Awesome teams also choose to build quality in from the very beginning. Lean tells us to fix any quality issues and the way we worked that caused them. Instead of debating which bugs we can skip over for later, we want to learn how to avoid them completely. As we're working toward this, we work in such a way that we do a bit of work, validate it, fix any issues that we find, and then iterate. The Agile Manifesto is clear that continuous attention to technical excellence and good design enhances agility [Manifesto].

Senior leadership within our organization can enable staff to be awesome individuals working on awesome teams by providing them with the authority and resources required for them to do their jobs, by building a safe culture and environment (see next principle), and by motivating them to excel. People are motivated by being provided with the autonomy to do their work, having opportunities to master their craft, and to do something that has purpose [Pink]. What would you rather have, staff who are motivated or demotivated?[1]

---

[1] If you think happy employees are expensive, wait until you try unhappy ones!

Principle: Context Counts

Every person is unique, with their own set of skills, preferences for work style, career goals, and learning styles. Every team is unique not only because it is composed of unique people, but also because it faces a unique situation. Our organization is also unique, even when there are other organizations that operate in the same marketplace that we do. For example, automobile manufacturers such as Ford, Audi, and Tesla all build the same category of product, yet it isn't much of a stretch to claim that they are very different companies. These observations—that people, teams, and organizations are all unique—lead us to a critical idea that our process and organization structure must be tailored for the situation that we currently face. In other words, context counts.

Figure 2.2, adapted from the Situation Context Framework (SCF) [SCF], shows that there are several context factors that affect how a team chooses its WoW. The factors are organized into two categories: factors which have a significant impact on our choice of life cycle (more on this in Chapter 6), and factors that motivate our choice of practices/strategies. The practice/strategy selection factors are a superset of the life-cycle-selection factors. For example, a team of eight people working in a common team room on a very complex domain problem in a life-critical regulatory situation will organize themselves differently, and will choose to follow different practices, than a team of 50 people spread out across a corporate campus on a complex problem in a nonregulatory situation. Although these two teams could be working for the same company, they could choose to work in very different ways.

There are several interesting implications of Figure 2.2. First, the further to the right on each selection factor, the greater the risk faced by a team. For example, it's much riskier to outsource than it is to build our own internal team. A team with a lower set of skills is a riskier proposition than a highly skilled team. A large team is a much riskier proposition than a small team. A life-critical regulatory situation is much riskier than a financial-critical situation, which in turn is riskier than facing no regulations at all. Second, because teams in different situations will need to choose to work in a manner that is appropriate for the situation that they face, to help them tailor their approach effectively, we need to give them choices. Third, anyone interacting with multiple teams needs to be flexible enough to work with each of those teams appropriately. For example, we will govern that small, colocated, life-critical team differently than the medium-sized team spread across the campus. Similarly, an enterprise architect (EA) who is supporting both teams will collaborate differently with each.

Scrum provides what used to be solid guidance for delivering value in an agile manner, but it is officially described by only a 19-page booklet [ScrumGuide]. Disciplined Agile recognizes that enterprise complexities require far more guidance, and thus provides a comprehensive reference tool kit for adapting our agile approach for our unique context in a straightforward manner. Being able to adapt our approach for our context with a variety of choices rather than standardizing on one method or framework is a good thing and we explore this further below.

Principle: Be Pragmatic

Many agilists are quite fanatical about following specific methods strictly. In fact, we have met many who say that to "do agile right," we need to have 5–9 people in a room, with the business (product owner) present at all times. The team should not be disturbed by people outside the team and

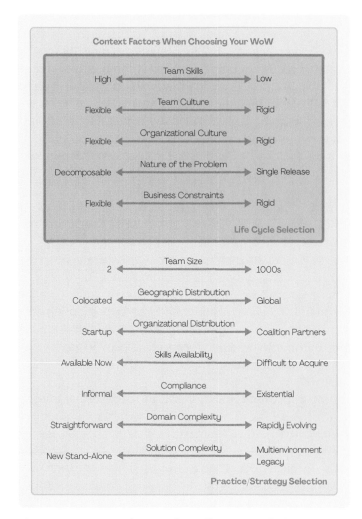

Figure 2.2 Context factors that affect WoW choices.

should be 100% dedicated to the project. However, in many established enterprises, such ideal conditions rarely exist. The reality is that we have to deal with many suboptimal situations, such as distributed teams, large team sizes, outsourcing, multiple team coordination, and part-time availability of stakeholders.

DA recognizes these realities, and rather than saying "we can't be agile" in these situations, we instead say: "Let's be pragmatic and aim to be as effective as we can be." Instead of prescribing "best practices," DA provides strategies for maximizing the benefits of agile despite certain necessary compromises being made. As such, DA is pragmatic, not purist in its guidance. DA provides guardrails to help us make better process choices, not strict rules that may not even be applicable given the context that we face.

Principle: Choice Is Good

Let's assume that our organization has multiple teams working in a range of situations, which in fact is the norm for all but the smallest of companies. How do we define a process that applies to each and every situation that covers the range of issues faced by each team? How do we keep it up to date as each team learns and evolves their approach? The answer is that we can't; documenting such a process is exponentially expensive. But does that mean we need to inflict the same prescriptive process on everyone? When we do that, we'll inflict process dissonance on our teams, decreasing their ability to be effective and increasing the chance that they'll invest resources in making it look as if they're following the process when in reality they're not. Or does this mean that we just have a "process free-for-all" and tell all our teams to figure it out on their own? Although this can work, it tends to be very expensive and time-consuming in practice. Even with coaching, each team is forced to invent or discover the practices and strategies that have been around for years, sometimes decades.

Developing new products, services, and software is a complex endeavor. That means we can never know for sure what's going to happen. There are many layers of activities going on at the same time and it's hard to see how each relates to the others. Systems are holistic and not understandable just by looking at their components. Instead, we must look at how the components of the system interact with each other. Consider a car, for example. While cars have components, the car itself is also about how the car's components interact with each other. For example, putting a bigger engine in a car might make the car unstable if the frame can't support it, or even dangerous if the brakes are no longer sufficient.

When making improvements to how we work, we must consider the following:

- How people interact with each other;
- How work being done in one part of the system affects the work in others;
- How people learn; and
- How people in the system interact with people outside of the system.

These interactions are unique to a particular organization. The principle of "context counts" means we must make intelligent choices based on the situation we are in. But how? We first recognize that we're not trying to figure out the best way to do things up front, but rather create a series of steps, each either making improvements on what we're doing or by learning something that will increase the likelihood of improvement the next time.

Each step in this series is presented as a hypothesis; that is, a conjecture that it will be an improvement if we can accomplish it. If we get improvement, we're happy and can go on to the next step. If we don't, we should ask why we didn't. Our efforts should lead to either improvement or learning, which then sets up the next improvement action. We can think of this as a scientific approach as we're trying actions and validating them. The cause may be that we took the wrong action, people didn't accept it, or it was beyond our capability.

Here's an example. Let's say that we see our people are multitasking a lot. Multitasking is usually caused by people working on too many things that they are not able to finish quickly. This causes them to go from one task to another and injects delays in their workflow as well as anyone depending upon them. How to stop this multitasking depends on the cause or causes of it. These are often clear or can be readily discerned. Even if we're not sure, trying something based on what's worked in similar situations in the past often achieves good results or learning. The salient aspect of DA is that we use practices that are germane to our situation, and to do that we need to know what practices exist that we could choose from.

Different contexts require different strategies. Teams need to be able to own their own process and to experiment to discover what works in practice for them given the situation that they face. As we learned in Chapter 1, DAD provides six life cycles for teams to choose from and 24 process goals that guide us toward choosing the right practices/strategies for our team given the situation that we face. Yes, it seems a bit complicated at first, but this approach proves to be a straightforward strategy to help address the complexities faced by solution delivery teams. Think of DAD, and DA in general, as the scaffolding that supports our efforts in choosing and evolving our WoW.

This choice-driven strategy is a middle way. At one extreme, we have prescriptive methods, which have their place, such as Scrum, Extreme Programming (XP), and SAFe®, which tell us one way to do things. Regardless of what the detractors of these methods claim, these methods/frameworks do in fact work quite well in some situations, and as long as we find ourselves in that situation, they'll work well for us. However, if we're not in the situation where a certain method fits, then it will likely do more harm than good. At the other extreme are creating our own methods by looking at our challenges, creating new practices based on principles, and trying them as experiments and learning as we go. This is how methods[2] that tell us to experiment and learn as we go developed their approach. This works well in practice, but can be very expensive, time-consuming, and can lead to significant inconsistencies between teams, which hampers our overall organizational process. Spotify® had the luxury of evolving their process within the context of a product company, common architecture, no technical debt, and a culture that they could grow rather than change—not to mention several in-house experts. DA sits between these two extremes; by taking this process-goal-driven approach, it provides process commonality between teams that is required at the organizational level, yet provides teams with flexible and straightforward guidance that is required to tailor and evolve their internal processes to address the context of the situation that they face. Teams can choose—from known strategies—the likely options to then experiment with, increasing the chance that they find something that works for them in practice. At a minimum, it at least makes it clear that they have choices, that there is more than the one way described by the prescriptive methods.

People are often surprised when we suggest that mainstream methods such as Scrum and Extreme Programming (XP) are prescriptive, but they are indeed. Scrum mandates a daily standup meeting (a scrum), no longer than 15 minutes, to which all team members must attend; that teams must have a retrospective at the end of each iteration (sprint); and that team size should not be more than nine people. Extreme Programming prescribes pair programming (two people sharing one keyboard) and test-driven development (TDD); granted, both of these are great practices in the right context. We are not suggesting that prescription is a bad thing, we're merely stating that it does exist.

In order to provide people with choices from which they can choose their way of working (WoW), DA has gathered strategies and put them into context from a wide array of sources. An important side effect of doing so is that it quickly forced us to take an agnostic approach.

---

[2] Spotify, like other methods, is a great source of potential ideas that we've mined in DA. We've particularly found their experimental approach to process improvement, which we've evolved into guided experiments (Chapter 1), to be useful. Unfortunately, many organizations try to adopt the Spotify method verbatim, which is exactly what the Spotify people tell us not to do. The Spotify method was great for them in their context several years ago. They are clear that if we are copying what they did then, that is not Spotify now. Our context, even if we happen to be a Swedish online music company, is different.

In DA, we've combined strategies from methods, frameworks, bodies of knowledge, books, our practical experiences helping organizations to improve, and many other sources. These sources use different terminology, sometimes overlap with each other, have different scopes, are based on different mindsets, and quite frankly often contradict each other. Chapter 3 goes into greater detail about how DA is a hybrid tool kit that provides agnostic process advice. As described earlier, leadership should encourage experimentation early in the interest of learning and improving as quickly as possible. However, we would suggest that by referencing the proven strategies in Disciplined Agile, we will make better choices for our context, speeding up process improvement through failing less. Better choices lead to better outcomes, earlier.

Principle: Optimize Flow

Although agile sprang from lean thinking in many ways, the principles of flow look to be transcending both. Don Reinertsen, in *Principles of Product Development Flow: 2nd Edition* [Reinertsen], provides more direct actions we can take to accelerate value realization. Looking at the flow of value enables teams to collaborate in a way as to effectively implement our organization's value streams. Although each team may be but one part of the value stream, they can see how they might align with others to maximize the realization of value.

The implication is that, as an organization, we need to optimize our overall workflow. DA supports strategies from agile, lean, and flow to do so:

1. **Optimize the whole.** DA teams work in an "enterprise-aware" manner. They realize that their team is one of many teams within their organization and, as a result, they should work in such a way as to do what is best for the overall organization and not just what is convenient for them. More importantly, they strive to streamline the overall process, to optimize the whole as the lean canon advises us to do. This includes finding ways to reduce the overall cycle time—the total time from the beginning to the end of the process to provide value to a customer [Reinertsen].
2. **Measure what counts.** Reinertsen's exhortation, "If you only quantify one thing, quantify the cost of delay," provides an across-the-organization view of what to optimize. "Cost of delay" is the cost to a business in value when a product is delayed. As an organization or as a value stream within an organization, and even at the team level, we will have outcomes that we want to achieve. Some of these outcomes will be customer-focused and some will be improvement-focused (often stemming from improving customer-focused outcomes). Our measures should be to assist in improving outcomes or in improving our ability to deliver better outcomes.
3. **Deliver small batches of work continuously at a sustainable pace.** Small batches of work not only enable us to get feedback faster, they enable us to not build things of lesser value, which often get thrown into a project. Dr. Goldratt, creator of Theory of Constraints (ToC), once remarked, "Often reducing batch size is all it takes to bring a system back into control" [Goldratt]. By delivering consumable solutions frequently, we can adjust what's really needed and avoid building things that aren't. By "consumable," we mean that it is usable, desirable, and functional (it fulfills its stakeholder's needs). "Solution" refers to something that may include software, hardware, changes to a business process, changes to the organizational structure of the people using the solution, and of course, any supporting documentation.
4. **Attend to delays by managing queues.** By attending to queues (work waiting to be done), we can identify bottlenecks and remove them using concepts from Lean, Theory of Constraints, and Kanban. This eliminates delays in workflow that create extra work.

5. **Improve continuously.** Optimizing flow requires continuous learning and improvement. The Evolve WoW process goal captures strategies to improve our team's work environment, our process, and our tooling infrastructure over time. Choosing our WoW is done on a continuous basis. This learning is not just about how we work, but what we are working on. Probably the most significant impact of Eric Ries' work in Lean Startup is the popularization of the experimentation mindset—the application of fundamental concepts of the scientific method to business. This mindset can be applied to process improvement following a guided continuous improvement (GCI) strategy that we described in Chapter 1. Validating our learnings is one of the guidelines of the DA mindset. Improve continuously is also one of the promises that disciplined agilists make to one another (see below).

6. **Prefer long-lived, dedicated product teams.** A very common trend in the agile community is the movement away from project teams to cross-functional product teams. This leads us to the next principle: Organize around products/services.

Principle: Organize Around Products/Services

There are several reasons why it is critical to organize around products and services, or more simply, offerings that we provide to our customers. What we mean by this is that we don't organize around job function, such as having a sales group, a business analysis group, a data analytics group, a vendor management group, a project management group, and so on. The problem with doing so is the overhead and time required to manage the work across these disparate teams and aligning the differing priorities of these teams. Instead, we build dedicated teams focused on delivering an offering for one or more customers. These teams will be cross-functional in that they include people with sales skills, business analysis skills, management skills, and so on.

Organizing around products/services enables us to identify and optimize the flows that count, which are value streams. We will find that a collection of related offerings will define a value stream that we provide to our customers, and this value stream will be implemented by the collection of teams for those offerings. The value stream layer of the DA tool kit, captured by the DA FLEX life cycle, was described in Chapter 1.

Organizing around products/services enables us to be laser-focused on delighting customers. Stephen Denning calls this the Law of the Customer, that everyone needs to be passionate about and focused on adding value to their customers [Denning]. Ideally, these are external customers, the people or organizations that our organization exists to serve. But sometimes these are also internal customers as well, other groups or people whom we are collaborating with so as to enable them to serve their customers more effectively.

Within a value stream, the industry has found that dedicated, cross-functional product teams that stay together over time are the most effective in practice [Kersten]. Having said that, there will always be project-based work as well. Chapter 6 shows that DA supports life cycles that are suited for project teams as well as dedicated product teams. Always remember, choice is good.

Principle: Enterprise Awareness

When people are enterprise aware, they are motivated to consider the overall needs of their organization, to ensure that what they're doing contributes positively to the goals of the organization and not just to the suboptimal goals of their team. This is an example of the lean principle of optimizing the whole. In this case, "the whole" is the organization, or at least the value stream, over local optimization at the team level.

Enterprise awareness positively changes people's behaviors in several important ways. First, they're more likely to work closely with enterprise professionals to seek their guidance. These people—such as enterprise architects, product managers, finance professionals, auditors, and senior executives—are responsible for our organization's business and technical strategies and for evolving our organization's overall vision. Second, enterprise-aware people are more likely to leverage and evolve existing assets within our organization, collaborating with the people responsible for those assets (such as data, code, and proven patterns or techniques) to do so. Third, they're more likely to adopt and follow common guidance, tailoring it where need be, thereby increasing overall consistency and quality. Fourth, they're more likely to share their learnings across teams, thereby speeding up our organization's overall improvement efforts. In fact, one of the process blades of DA, Continuous Improvement, is focused on helping people to share learnings. Fifth, enterprise-aware people are more likely to be willing to work in a transparent manner, although they expect reciprocity from others.

There is the potential for negative consequences as well. Some people believe that enterprise awareness demands absolute consistency and process adherence by teams, not realizing that context counts and that every team needs to make their own process decisions (within bounds or what's commonly called "guardrails"). Enterprise awareness can lead some people into a state of "analysis paralysis," where they are unable to make a decision because they're overwhelmed by the complexity of the organization.

We Promise To

Because disciplined agilists believe in the principles of DA, they promise to adopt behaviors that enable them to work both within their team and with others more effectively. These promises are designed to be synergistic in practice, and they have positive feedback cycles between them. The promises of the DA mindset are:

- Create psychological safety and embrace diversity.
- Accelerate value realization.
- Collaborate proactively.
- Make all work and workflow visible.

- Improve predictability.
- Keep workloads within capacity.
- Improve continuously.

Promise: Create Psychological Safety and Embrace Diversity

Psychological safety means being able to show and employ oneself without fear of negative consequences of status, career, or self-worth—we should be comfortable being ourselves in our work setting. A 2015 study at Google found that successful teams provide psychological safety for team members, that team members are able to depend on one another, there is structure and clarity around roles and responsibilities, and people are doing work that is both meaningful and impactful to them [Google].

Psychological safety goes hand in hand with diversity, which is the recognition that everyone is unique and can add value in different ways. The dimensions of personal uniqueness include, but are not limited to, race, ethnicity, gender, sexual orientation, agility, physical abilities, socioeconomic status, religious beliefs, political beliefs, and other ideological beliefs. Diversity is critical to a team's success because it enables greater innovation. The more diverse our team, the better our ideas will be, the better our work will be, and the more we'll learn from each other.

There are several strategies that enable us to nurture psychological safety and diversity within a team:

1. **Be respectful.** Everyone is different, with different experiences and different preferences. None of us is the smartest person in the room. Respect what other people know that we don't and recognize that they have a different and important point of view.
2. **Be humble.** In many ways, this is key to having a learning mindset and to being respectful.
3. **Be ethical and trustworthy.** People will feel safer working and interacting with us if they trust us. Trust is built over time through a series of actions and can be broken instantly by one action.
4. **Make it safe to fail.** There is a catchy phrase in the agile world called "fail fast." We prefer Al Shalloway's advice, "Make it safe to fail so you can learn fast." The idea is to not hesitate to try something, even if it may fail. But the focus should be on learning safely and quickly. Note that "safely" refers both to psychological safety and the safety of our work. As we learned in Chapter 1, the aim of guided continuous improvement (GCI) is to try out new ways of working (WoW) with the expectation that they will work for us, while being prepared to learn from our experiment if it fails.

Promise: Accelerate Value Realization

An important question to ask is: What is value? Customer value—something that benefits the end customer who consumes the product/service that our team helps to provide—is what agilists typically focus on. This is clearly important, but in Disciplined Agile we're very clear that teams have a range of stakeholders, including external end customers. So, shouldn't we provide value to them as well?

Mark Schwartz, in *The Art of Business Value*, distinguishes between two types of value: customer value and business value [Schwartz]. Business value addresses the issue that some things are of benefit to our organization and perhaps only indirectly to our customers. For example, investing in enterprise architecture, reusable infrastructure, and sharing innovations across our organization offers the potential to improve consistency, quality, reliability, and reduce cost over the long term. These things have great value to our organization but may have little direct impact on customer value. Yet, working in an enterprise-aware manner such as this is clearly a very smart thing to do.

There are several ways that we can accelerate value realization:

1. **Work on small, high-value items.** By working on the most valuable thing right now, we increase the overall return on investment (ROI) of our efforts. By working on small things and releasing them quickly, we reduce the overall cost of delay and our feedback cycle by getting our work into the hands of stakeholders quickly. This is a very common strategy in the agile community and is arguably a fundamental of agile.
2. **Reuse existing assets.** Our organization very likely has a lot of great stuff that we can take advantage of, such as existing tools, systems, sources of data, standards, and many other assets. But we need to choose to look for them, we need to be supported in getting access to them and in learning about them, and we may need to do a bit of work to improve upon the assets to make them fit our situation. One of the guidelines of the DA mindset, described later in this chapter, is to leverage and enhance organizational assets.
3. **Collaborate with other teams.** An easy way to accelerate value realization is to work with others to get the job done. Remember the old saying: Many hands make light work.

Promise: Collaborate Proactively

Disciplined agilists strive to add value to the whole, not just to their individual work or to the team's work. The implication is that we want to collaborate both within our team and with others outside our team, and we also want to be proactive doing so. Waiting to be asked is passive, observing that someone needs help and then volunteering to do so is proactive. We have observed that are three important opportunities for proactive collaboration:

1. **Within our team.** We should always be focused on being awesome and on working with and helping out our fellow team members. So if we see that someone is overloaded with work or is struggling to work through something, don't just wait to be asked but instead volunteer to help out.
2. **With our stakeholders.** Awesome teams have a very good working relationship with their stakeholders, collaborating with them to ensure that what they do is what the stakeholders actually need.
3. **Across organizational boundaries.** In Chapter 1, we discussed how an organization is a complex adaptive system (CAS) of teams interacting with other teams.

Promise: Make All Work and Workflow Visible

Disciplined Agile teams—and individual team members—make all their work and how they are working visible to others.[3] This is often referred to as "radical transparency" and the idea is that we should be open and honest with others. Not everyone is comfortable with this.

---

[3] This, of course, may be constrained by the need to maintain secrecy, resulting either from competitive or regulatory concerns.

Organizations with traditional methods have a lot of watermelon projects—green on the outside and red on the inside—by which we mean that they claim to be doing well even though they're really in trouble. Transparency is critical for both supporting effective governance and for enabling collaboration as people are able to see what others are currently working on.

Disciplined agile teams will often make their work visible at both the individual level as well as the team level. It is critical to focus on our work in process, which is more than the work in progress. Work in progress is what we are currently working on. Work in process is our work in progress plus any work that is queued up waiting for us to get to it. Disciplined agilists focus on work in process as a result.

Disciplined teams make their workflow visible, and thus have explicit workflow policies so that everyone knows how everyone else is working. This supports collaboration because people have agreements as to how they are going to work together. It also supports process improvement because it enables us to understand what is happening and thereby increases the chance that we can detect where we have potential issues. It is important that we are both agnostic and pragmatic in the way that we work, as we want to do the best that we can in the context that we face.

Promise: Improve Predictability

Disciplined teams strive to improve their predictability to enable them to collaborate and self-organize more effectively, and thereby to increase the chance that they will fulfill any commitments that they make to their stakeholders. Many of the earlier promises we have made work toward improving predictability. To see how to improve predictability, it is often useful to see what causes unpredictability, such as technical debt and overloaded team members, and to then attack those challenges.

Common strategies to improve predictability include:

- **Pay down technical debt.** Technical debt refers to the implied cost of future refactoring or rework to improve the quality of an asset to make it easy to maintain and extend. When we have significant technical debt, it becomes difficult to predict how much effort work will be—working with high-quality assets is much easier than working with low-quality assets. Because most technical debt is hidden (we don't really know what invokes that source code we're just about to change or we don't know what's really behind that wall we're about to pull down as we renovate our kitchen), it often presents us with unpredictable surprises when we get into the work. Paying down technical debt, described by the Improve Quality process goal, is an important strategy for increasing the predictability of our work.
- **Respect work-in-process (WIP) limits.** When people are working close to or at their maximum capacity then it becomes difficult to predict how long something will take to accomplish. Those 2 days' worth of work might take us 3 months to accomplish because we either let it sit in our work queue for 3 months or we do a bit of the work at a time over a 3-month period. Worse yet, the more loaded someone becomes, the more their feedback cycles will increase in length, generating even more work for them (see below) and thus increasing their workload further. So we want to keep workloads within capacity, another one of our promises.

- **Adopt a test-first approach.** With a test-first approach, we think through how we will test something before we build it. This has the advantage that our tests both specify as well as validate our work, thereby doing double duty, which will very likely motivate us to create a higher-quality work product. It also increases our predictability because we will have a better understanding of what we're working on before actually working on it. There are several common practices that take a test-first approach, including acceptance test-driven development (ATDD) [ExecutableSpecs], where we capture detailed requirements via working acceptance tests, and test-driven development (TDD) [Beck; TDD], where our design is captured as working developer tests.
- **Reduce feedback cycles.** A feedback cycle is the amount of time between doing something and getting feedback about it. For example, if we write a memo and then send it to someone to see what they think, and it then takes 4 days for them to get back to us, the feedback cycle is 4 days long. But, if we work collaboratively and write the memo together, a technique called pairing, then the feedback cycle is on the order of seconds because they can see what we type and discuss it as we're typing. Short feedback cycles enable us to act quickly to improve the quality of our work, thereby improving our predictability and increasing the chance that we will delight our customers. Long feedback cycles are problematic because the longer it takes to get feedback, the greater the chance that any problems we have in our work will be built upon, thereby increasing the cost of addressing any problems because now we need to fix the original problem and anything that extends it. Long feedback cycles also increase the chance that the requirement for the work will evolve, either because something changed in the environment or because someone simply changed their mind about what they want. In both cases, the longer feedback cycle results in more work for us to do and thereby increases our workload (as discussed earlier).

Promise: Keep Workloads Within Capacity

Going beyond capacity is problematic from both a personal and a productivity point of view. At the personal level, overloading a person or team will often increase the frustration of the people involved. Although it may motivate some people to work harder in the short term, it will cause burnout in the long term, and it may even motivate people to give up and leave because the situation seems hopeless to them. From a productivity point of view, overloading causes multitasking, which increases overall overhead. We can keep workloads within capacity by:

- **Working on small batches.** Having small batches of work enables us to focus on getting the small batch done and then move on to the next small batch.
- **Having properly formed teams.** Teams that are cross-functional and sufficiently staffed increase our ability to keep workload within capacity because it reduces dependencies on others. The more dependencies we have, the less predictable our work becomes and therefore is harder to organize.
- **Take a flow perspective.** By looking at the overall workflow we are part of, we can identify where we are over capacity by looking for bottlenecks where work is queuing up. We can then adjust our WoW to alleviate the bottleneck, perhaps by shifting people from one activity to another where we need more capacity, or improving our approach to the activity where we have the bottleneck. Our aim, of course, is to optimize flow across the entire value stream that we are part of, not to just locally optimize our own workflow.
- **Use a pull system.** One of the advantages of pulling work when we are ready is that we can manage our own workload level.

Promise: Improve Continuously

The really successful organizations—Apple, Amazon, eBay, Facebook, Google, and more—got that way through continuous improvement. They realized that to remain competitive, they needed to constantly look for ways to improve their processes, the outcomes that they were delivering to their customers, and their organizational structures. This is why these organizations adopt a kaizen-based approach of improving via small changes. In Chapter 1, we learned that we can do even better than that by taking a guided continuous improvement (GCI) approach that leverages the knowledge base contained within the DA tool kit.

Continuous improvement requires us to have agreement on what we're improving. We've observed that teams that focus on improving on the way that they fulfill the promises described here, including improving on the way that they improve, tend to improve faster than those that don't. Our team clearly benefits by increasing safety and diversity, improving collaboration, improving predictability, and keeping their workload within capacity. Our organization also benefits from these things when we improve upon the other promises.

We Follow These Guidelines

To fulfill the promises that disciplined agilists make, they will choose to follow a collection of guidelines that make them more effective in the way that they work. The guidelines of the DA mindset are:

1. Validate our learnings.
2. Apply design thinking.
3. Attend to relationships through the value stream.
4. Create effective environments that foster joy.
5. Change culture by improving the system.
6. Create semi-autonomous, self-organizing teams.
7. Adopt measures to improve outcomes.
8. Leverage and enhance organizational assets.

Guideline: Validate Our Learnings

The only way to become awesome is to experiment with, and then adopt where appropriate, a new WoW. In the GCI workflow, after we experiment with a new way of working, we assess how well it worked, an approach called validated learning. Hopefully, we discover that the new WoW works for us in our context, but we may also discover that it doesn't. Either way, we've validated what we've learned. Being willing and able to experiment is critical to our process-improvement efforts. Remember Mark Twain's aphorism: "It ain't what you don't know that gets you into trouble. It's what you know for sure that just ain't so."

Validated learning isn't just for process improvement. We should also apply this strategy to the product/service (offering) that we are providing to our customers. We can build in thin slices, make changes available to our stakeholders, and then assess how well that change works in practice. We can do this through demoing our offering to our stakeholders or, better yet, releasing our changes to actual end users and measuring whether they benefited from these changes.

Guideline: Apply Design Thinking

Delighting customers requires us to recognize that our work is to create operational value streams for our customers that are designed with them in mind. This requires design thinking on our part. Design thinking means to be empathetic to the customer, to first try to understand their environment and needs before developing a solution. Design thinking represents a fundamental shift from building systems from our perspective to creatively solving customer problems and, better yet, fulfilling needs they didn't even know they had.

Design thinking is an exploratory approach that should be used to iteratively explore a problem space and identify potential solutions for it. Design thinking has its roots in user-centered design as well as usage-centered design, both of which influenced Agile Modeling, one of many methods that the DA tool kit adopts practices from. In Chapter 6, we will learn that DA includes the Exploratory life cycle, which is specifically used for exploring a new problem space.

Guideline: Attend to Relationships Through the Value Stream

One of greatest strengths of the Agile Manifesto is its first value: Individuals and interactions over processes and tools. Another strength is the focus on teams in the principles behind the manifesto. However, the unfortunate side effect of this takes the focus away from the interactions between people on different teams or even in different organizations. Our experience, and we believe this is what the authors of the manifesto meant, is that the interactions between the people doing the work are what is key, regardless of whether or not they are part of the team. So, if a product manager needs to work closely with our organization's data analytics team to gain a better understanding of what is going on in the marketplace, and our strategy team to help put those observations into context, then we want to ensure that these interactions are effective. We need to proactively collaborate between these teams to support the overall work at hand.

Caring for and maintaining healthy interactive processes is important for the people involved and should be supported and enabled by our organizational leadership. In fact, there is a leadership strategy called middle-up-down management [Nonaka], where management looks "up" the value stream to identify what is needed, enables the team to fulfill that need, and works with the teams downstream to coordinate work effectively. The overall goal is to coordinate locally in a manner that supports optimizing the overall workflow.

Guideline: Create Effective Environments That Foster Joy

To paraphrase the Agile Manifesto, awesome teams are built around motivated individuals who are given the environment and support required to fulfill their objectives. Part of being awesome is having fun and being joyful. We want working in our company to be a great experience so we can attract and keep the best people. Done right, work is play.

We can make our work more joyful by creating an environment that allows us to work together well. A key strategy to achieve this is to allow teams to be self-organizing—to let them choose and evolve their own WoW, organizational structure, and working environments. Teams must do so in an enterprise-aware manner—meaning we need to collaborate with other teams, and there are organizational procedures and standards we must follow and constraints on what we can do.

The job of leadership is to provide a good environment for teams to start in and then to support and enable teams to improve as they learn over time.

Guideline: Change Culture by Improving the System

Peter Drucker is famous for saying that "culture eats strategy for breakfast." This is something that the agile community has taken to heart, and this philosophy is clearly reflected in the people-oriented nature of the Agile Manifesto. While culture is important, and culture change is a critical component of any organization's agile transformation, the unfortunate reality is that we can't change it directly. This is because culture is a reflection of the management system in place, so to change our culture, we need to evolve our overall system.

From a systems point of view, the system is both the sum of its components plus how they interact with each other [Meadows]. In the case of an organization, the components are the teams/groups within it and the tools and other assets, both digital and physical, that they work with. The interactions are the collaborations of the people involved, which are driven by the roles and responsibilities that they take on and their WoW. To improve a system, we need to evolve both its components and the interactions between those components in lock step.

To improve the components of our organizational system, we need to evolve our team structures and the tools/assets that we use to do our work. The next DA mindset guideline, create semi-autonomous, self-organizing teams, addresses the team side of this. The Improve Quality process goal captures options for improving the quality of our infrastructure, which tends to be a long-term endeavor requiring significant investment. To improve the interactions between components, which is the focus of this book, we need to evolve the roles and responsibilities of the people working on our teams and enable them to evolve their WoW.

To summarize, if we improve the system, then culture change will follow. To ensure that culture change is positive, we need to take a validated learning approach to these improvements.

Guideline: Create Semi-Autonomous, Self-Organizing Teams

Organizations are complex adaptive systems (CAS) made up of a network of teams or, if you will, a team of teams. Although mainstream agile implores us to create "whole teams" that have all of the skills and resources required to achieve the outcomes that they've been tasked with, the reality is that no team is an island unto itself. Autonomous teams would be ideal, but there are always dependencies on other teams upstream that we are part of, as well as downstream from us. And, of course, there are dependencies between offerings (products or services) that necessitate the teams responsible for them to collaborate. This network-of-teams organizational structure is being recommended by Stephen Denning in his Law of the Network [Denning], Mik Kersten in his recommendation to shift from project to product teams [Kersten], John Kotter in *Accelerate* [Kotter], Stanley McChrystal in his team-of-teams strategy [MCSF], and many others.

Teams will proactively collaborate with other teams on a regular basis, one of the promises of the DA mindset. Awesome teams are as whole as possible—they are cross-functional; have the skills, resources, and authority required to be successful; and team members themselves tend to be cross-functional generalizing specialists. Furthermore, they are organized around the products/services offered by the value stream they are part of. Interestingly, when we have teams dedicated to business stakeholders, budgeting becomes much simpler because we just need to budget for the people aligned with each product/service.

Creating semi-autonomous teams is a great start, but self-organization within the context of the value stream is also something to attend to. Teams will be self-organizing, but they must do so within the context of the overall workflow that they are part of. Remember the principles of optimize flow and enterprise awareness, in that teams must strive to do what's right for the overall organization, not just what is convenient for them. When other teams also work in such a way, we are all much better for it.

Guideline: Adopt Measures to Improve Outcomes

When it comes to measurement, context counts. What are we hoping to improve? Quality? Time to market? Staff morale? Customer satisfaction? Combinations thereof? Every person, team, and organization has their own improvement priorities, and their own ways of working, so they will have their own set of measures that they gather to provide insight into how they're doing and, more importantly, how to proceed. And these measures evolve over time as their situation and priorities evolve. The implication is that our measurement strategy must be flexible and fit for purpose, and it will vary across teams. The Govern Team process goal provides several strategies, including goal question metric (GQM) [GQM] and objectives and key results (OKRs) [Doer], that promote context-driven metrics.

Metrics should be used by a team to provide insights into how they work and provide visibility to senior leadership to govern the team effectively. When done right, metrics will lead to better decisions, which in turn will lead to better outcomes. When done wrong, our measurement strategy will increase the bureaucracy faced by the team, will be a drag on their productivity, and will provide inaccurate information to whomever is trying to govern the team. Here are several heuristics to consider when deciding on the approach to measuring our team:

- Start with outcomes.
- Measure what is directly related to delivering value.
- There is no "one way" to measure; teams need fit-for-purpose metrics.
- Every metric has strengths and weaknesses.
- Use metrics to motivate, not to compare.
- We get what we measure.
- Teams use metrics to self-organize.
- Measure outcomes at the team level.
- Each team needs a unique set of metrics.
- Measure to improve; we need to measure our pain so we can see our gain.
- Have common metric categories across teams, not common metrics.
- Trust but verify.
- Don't manage to the metrics.
- Automate wherever possible so as to make the metrics ungameable.
- Prefer trends over scalars.
- Prefer leading over trailing metrics.
- Prefer pull over push.

Guideline: Leverage and Enhance Organizational Assets

Our organization has many assets—information systems, information sources, tools, templates, procedures, learnings, and other things—that our team could adopt to improve our effectiveness. We may not only choose to adopt these assets, we may also find that we can improve them to make them better for us as well as other teams that also choose to work with these assets. This guideline is important for several reasons:

1. **A lot of good work has been done before.** There is a wide range of assets within our organization that our team can leverage. Sometimes we will discover that we need to first evolve the existing asset so that it meets our needs, which often proves faster and less expensive than building it from scratch.
2. **A lot of good work continues around us.** Our organization is a network of semi-autonomous, self-organizing teams. We can work with and learn from these teams, proactively collaborating with them, thereby accelerating value realization. The enterprise architecture team can help point us in the right direction and we can help them learn how well their strategies work when applied in practice. Stephen Denning stresses the need for the business operations side of our organization, such as vendor management, finance, and people management, to support the teams executing the value streams of our organization [Denning]. We must work and learn together in an enterprise-aware manner if we are to delight our customers.
3. **We can reduce overall technical debt.** The unfortunate reality is that many organizations struggle under significant technical debt loads, as we discussed earlier. By choosing to reuse existing assets, and investing in paying down some of the technical debt that we run into when doing so, we'll slowly dig our way out of the technical debt trap that we find ourselves in.
4. **We can provide greater value quicker.** Increased reuse enables us to focus on implementing new functionality to delight our customers instead of just reinventing what we're already offering them. By paying down technical debt, we increase the underlying quality of the infrastructure upon which we're building, enabling us to deliver new functionality faster over time.
5. **We can support others.** Just like our team collaborates with and learns from other teams, so do those other teams collaborate and learn from us. At the organizational level, we can enhance this through the creation of centers of excellence (CoEs) and communities of practice (CoPs) to capture and share learnings across the organization [CoE; CoP].

And a Few More Great Philosophies

Here are a few philosophies that we've seen work well in practice for disciplined agilists:

1. **If it's hard, do it more often.** You believe system integration testing (SIT) is hard? Instead of pushing it to the end of the life cycle, like traditionalists do, find a way to do it every single iteration. Then find a way to do it every single day. Doing hard things more often forces us to find ways, often through automation, to make them easier.
2. **If it's scary, do it more often.** We're afraid to evolve a certain piece of code? We're afraid to get feedback from stakeholders because they may change their minds? Then let's do it more often and find ways to overcome what we fear. Find ways to avoid the negative outcomes, or to turn them positive. Fix that code. Make it easier to evolve our solution. Help those stakeholders understand the implications of the decisions they're making.

3. **Keep asking why.** To truly understand something, we need to ask why it happened, why it works that way, or why it's important to others. Then ask why again, and again, and again. Toyota calls this practice five whys analysis [Liker], but don't treat five as a magic number. We keep asking why until we get to the root cause.

4. **Learn something every day.** Disciplined agilists strive to learn something every day. Perhaps it's something about the domain they're working in. Perhaps it's something about the technologies, or something about their tools. Perhaps it's a new practice, or a new way to perform a practice. There are a lot of learning opportunities before us. Take them.

In Summary

How can we summarize the Disciplined Agile mindset? Simon Powers sums up the mindset in terms of three core beliefs [Powers]. These beliefs are:

1. **The complexity belief.** Many of the problems that we face are complex adaptive problems, meaning that by trying to solve these problems we change the nature of the problems themselves.

2. **The people belief.** Individuals are both independent from and dependent on their teams and organizations. Human beings are interdependent. Given the right environment (safety, respect, diversity, and inclusion) and a motivating purpose, it is possible for trust and self-organization to arise. For this to happen, it is necessary to treat everyone with unconditional positive regard.

3. **The proactive belief.** Proactivity is found in the relentless pursuit of improvement.

We find these beliefs compelling. In many ways, they summarize the fundamental motivations behind why we need to choose our WoW. Because we face a unique context, we need to tailor our WoW, and in doing so, we change the situation that we face that also requires us to learn and evolve our WoW. The people belief motivates us to find a WoW that enables us to work together effectively and safely, and the proactive belief reflects the idea that we should continuously learn and improve.

Mindset Is Only the Beginning

The Disciplined Agile mindset provides a solid foundation from which our organization can become agile, but it is only a foundation. Our fear is that too many inexperienced coaches are dumbing down agile, hoping to focus on the concepts overviewed in this chapter. It's a good start, but it doesn't get the job done in practice. It isn't sufficient to "be agile," we also need to know how to "do agile." It's wonderful when someone wants to work in a collaborative, respectful manner, but if they don't actually know how to do the work, they're not going to get much done. Software development and, more importantly, solution delivery are complex—we need to know what we're doing.

Chapter 3

Disciplined Agile Delivery (DAD) in a Nutshell

Discipline is doing what you know needs to be done,
even if you don't want to do it. –Unknown

Key Points in This Chapter

- DAD is the delivery portion of the Disciplined Agile (DA) tool kit—it is not just another methodology.
- If you are using Scrum, XP, or Kanban, you are already using variations of a subset of DAD.
- DAD provides six life cycles to choose from; it doesn't prescribe a single way of working—choice is good.
- DAD addresses key enterprise concerns.
- DAD does the process heavy lifting so that you don't have to.
- DAD shows how agile development works from beginning to end.
- DAD provides a flexible foundation from which to tactically scale mainstream methods.
- It is easy to get started with DAD.
- You can start with your existing WoW and then apply DAD to improve it gradually. You don't need to make a risky "big bang" change.

Many organizations start their agile journey by adopting Scrum because it describes a good strategy for leading agile software teams. However, Scrum is a very small part of what is required to deliver sophisticated solutions to your stakeholders. Invariably, teams need to look to other methods to fill in the process gaps that Scrum purposely ignores, and Scrum is very clear about this. When looking at other methods, there is considerable overlap and conflicting terminology that can be confusing to practitioners as well as outside stakeholders. Worse yet, people don't always know where to look for advice or even know what issues they need to consider.

To address these challenges, Disciplined Agile Delivery (DAD) provides a more cohesive approach to agile solution delivery. DAD is a people-first, learning-oriented, hybrid agile approach to IT solution delivery. These are the critical aspects of DAD:

1. **People first.** People, and the way we work together, are the primary determinants of success for a solution delivery team. DAD supports a robust set of roles, rights, and responsibilities that you can tailor to meet the needs of your situation.

2. **Hybrid.** DAD is a hybrid tool kit that puts great ideas from Scrum, SAFe, Spotify, Agile Modeling (AM), Extreme Programming (XP), Unified Process (UP), Kanban, Lean Software Development, and several other methods into context.
3. **Full-delivery life cycle.** DAD addresses the full-delivery life cycle, from team initiation all the way to delivering a solution to your end users.
4. **Support for multiple life cycles.** DAD supports agile, lean, continuous delivery, exploratory, and large-team versions of the life cycle. DAD doesn't prescribe a single life cycle because it recognizes that one process approach does not fit all. Chapter 6 explores life cycles in greater detail, providing advice for selecting the right one to start with and then how to evolve from one to another over time.
5. **Complete.** DAD shows how development, modeling, architecture, management, requirements/ outcomes, documentation, governance, and other strategies fit together in a streamlined whole. DAD does the "process heavy lifting" that other methods leave up to you.
6. **Context-sensitive.** DAD promotes what we call a goal-driven or outcome-driven approach. In doing so, DAD provides contextual advice regarding viable alternatives and their trade-offs, enabling you to tailor DAD to effectively address the situation in which you find yourself. By describing what works, what doesn't work, and more importantly why, DAD helps you to increase your chance of adopting strategies that will work for you and do so in a streamlined manner. Remember the DA principle: Context counts.
7. **Consumable solutions over working software.** Potentially shippable software is a good start, but what we really need are consumable solutions that delight our customers.
8. **Self-organization with appropriate governance.** Agile and lean teams are self-organizing, which means that the people who do the work are the ones who plan and estimate it. But that doesn't mean they can do whatever they want. They must still work in an enterprise-aware manner that reflects the priorities of their organization, and to do that they will need to be governed appropriately by senior leadership. The Govern Team process goal describes options for doing exactly that.

This chapter provides a brief overview of DAD, with the details coming in later chapters.

What's New With DAD?

For existing DAD practitioners, there are several exciting changes that you'll see in this book compared to *Disciplined Agile Delivery: A Practitioner's Guide to Agile Software Delivery in the Enterprise* [AmblerLines2012]. We've made these changes based on our work at dozens of organizations worldwide and, more importantly, from the input we've received from a myriad of practitioners. These changes are:

1. **The process goals have been refactored.** Over the past several years, we've renamed some goals, introduced a new goal, and combined two pairs of goals. We believe it will make the goals more understandable.
2. **Every goal has been updated.** We've learned a lot over the last several years, a lot of great techniques have appeared, and we've applied older techniques in new situations. We've been posting updates to the goals online at PMI.org/disciplined-agile and in our courseware, but this is the first time we've captured all of the updates in print.
3. **All of the goals are captured visually.** This is the first book to capture all of DAD's goal diagrams. We introduced the goal diagrams after the original 2012 book came out.

4. **New and updated life cycles.** We've explicitly introduced the Program life cycle (we had described it in terms of team structure before) and the Exploratory life cycle. We've also introduced both agile and lean versions of what we used to call the Continuous Delivery life cycle.
5. **Advice for applying the tool kit in practice.** A big difference you'll see in this book is much more advice for how to apply DA in practice. This advice reflects the additional years of working with organizations around the world to adopt Disciplined Agile strategies.

People First: Roles, Rights, and Responsibilities

Figure 3.1 shows the potential roles that people will fill on DAD teams, and Chapter 4 describes them in detail. The roles are organized into two categories: primary roles that we find are critical to the success of any agile team and supporting roles that appear as needed.

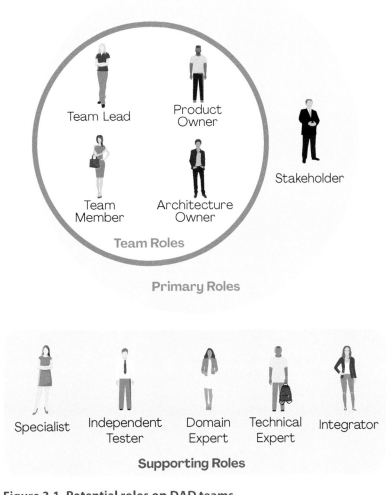

Figure 3.1 Potential roles on DAD teams.

The primary roles are:

- **Team lead.** This person leads the team, helping the team to be successful. This may be a senior scrum master, project manager, or functional manager.
- **Product owner (PO).** A product owner is responsible for working with stakeholders to identify the work to be done, prioritize that work, help the team to understand the stakeholders' needs, and help the team interact effectively with stakeholders [ScrumGuide].
- **Architecture owner (AO).** An architecture owner guides the team through architecture and design decisions, working closely with the team lead and product owner when doing so [AgileModeling].
- **Team member.** Team members work together to produce the solution. Ideally, team members are generalizing specialists, or working on becoming so, who are often referred to as cross-skilled people. A generalizing specialist is someone with one or more specialties (such as testing, analysis, programming, etc.) and a broad knowledge of solution delivery and the domain they are working in [GenSpec].
- **Stakeholder.** A stakeholder is someone who will be affected by the work of the team, including but not limited to end users, support engineers, operations staff, financial people, auditors, enterprise architects, and senior leadership. Some agile methods call this role customer.

The supporting roles are:

- **Specialist.** Although most team members will be generalizing specialists, or at least striving to be so, we sometimes have specialists on teams when called for. User experience (UX) and security experts are specialists who may be on a team when there is significant user interface (UI) development or security concerns, respectively. Sometimes business analysts are needed to support product owners in dealing with a complex domain or geographically distributed stakeholders. Furthermore, roles from other parts of the DA tool kit such as enterprise architects, portfolio managers, reuse engineers, operations engineers, and others are considered specialists from a DAD point of view.
- **Independent tester.** Although the majority of testing, if not all of it, should be performed by the team, there can be a need for an independent test team at scale. Common scenarios requiring independent testers include: regulatory compliance that requires that some testing occur outside of the team, and a large program (a team of teams) working on a complex solution that has significant integration challenges.
- **Domain expert.** A domain expert, sometimes called a subject matter expert (SME), is someone with deep knowledge in a given domain or problem space. They often work with the team or product owners to share their knowledge and experience.
- **Technical expert.** This is someone with deep technical expertise who works with the team for a short time to help them overcome a specific technical challenge. For example, an operational database administrator (DBA) may work with the team to help them set up, configure, and learn the fundamentals of a database.
- **Integrator.** Also called a system integrator, they will often support independent testers who need to perform system integration testing (SIT) of a complex solution or collection of solutions.

Everyone on agile teams has rights and responsibilities. Everyone. For example, everyone has the right to be given respect, but they also have the responsibility to give respect to others.

Disciplined Agile® (DA™)

Figure 3.2 DAD is an agnostic hybrid of great ideas.

Furthermore, each role on an agile team has specific additional responsibilities that they must fulfill. Rights and responsibilities are also covered in detail in Chapter 4.

A Hybrid of Great Ideas

We like to say that DAD does the heavy process lifting so that you don't have to. What we mean by that is that is we've mined the various methods, frameworks, and other sources to identify potential practices and strategies that your team may want to experiment with and adopt. We put these techniques into context, exploring fundamental concepts such as what are the advantages and disadvantages of the technique, when would you apply the technique, when wouldn't you apply the technique, and to what extent would you apply it? Answers to these questions are critical when a team is choosing its WoW.

Figure 3.2 indicates some of the methodologies and frameworks that we've mined for techniques. For example, XP is the source of technical practices such as test-driven development (TDD), refactoring, and pair programming to name a few. Scrum is the source of strategies such as product backlogs, sprint/iteration planning, daily coordination meetings, and more. Agile Modeling gives us model storming, initial architecture envisioning, continuous documentation, and active stakeholder participation. Where these methods go into detail about these individual techniques, the focus of DAD, and DA in general, is to put them into context and to help you choose the right strategy at the right time.

Choice Is Good: Process Goals

DAD includes a collection of 24 process goals, or process outcomes if you like, as Figure 3.3 shows. Each goal is described as a collection of decision points, issues that your team needs to determine whether they need to address and, if so, how they will do so. Potential practices/strategies for addressing a decision point, which can be combined in many cases, are presented as lists. Goal diagrams, an example is shown in Figure 3.4, are similar conceptually to mind maps, albeit with the extension of the arrow to represent the relative effectiveness of options in some cases.

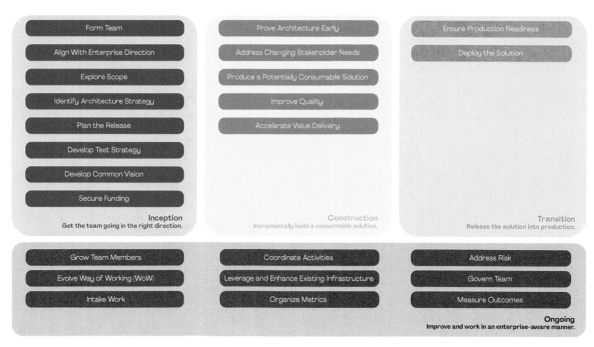

Figure 3.3 The process goals of DAD.

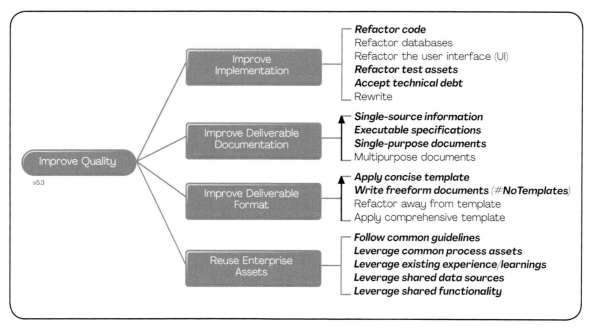

Figure 3.4 The Improve Quality process goal diagram.

Goal diagrams are, in effect, guides to help a team to choose the best strategies that they are capable of doing right now given their skills, culture, and situation. Chapter 5 explores DAD's goal-driven approach and the Disciplined Agile Browser [DABrowser] provides supporting details.

Choice Is Good: Multiple Life Cycle Support

Life cycles put an order to the activities that a team performs to build a solution. In effect, they organize the techniques that we apply to get the work done. Because solution delivery teams find themselves in a range of different situations, they need to be able to choose a life cycle that best fits the context that they face. You can see in Figure 3.5 that DAD supports six life cycles:

1. **Agile.** This is a Scrum-based life cycle for solution delivery projects.
2. **Lean.** This is a Kanban-based life cycle for solution delivery projects.
3. **Continuous Delivery: Agile.** This is a Scrum-based life cycle for long-standing teams.
4. **Continuous Delivery: Lean.** This is a Kanban-based life cycle for long-standing teams.
5. **Exploratory.** This is a Lean Startup-based life cycle for running experiments with potential customers to discover what they actually want. This life cycle supports a design thinking approach, as described in Chapter 2.
6. **Program.** This is a life cycle for a team of agile or lean teams.

Chapter 6 describes the six DAD life cycles in detail, as well as the traditional life cycle, and provides advice for when to choose each one.

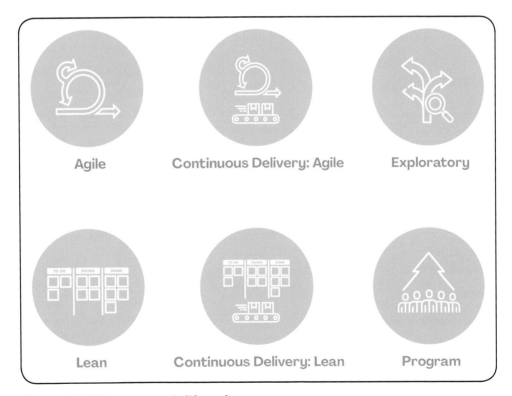

Figure 3.5 DAD supports six life cycles.

Consumable Solutions Over Working Software

The Agile Manifesto suggests that we measure progress based upon "working software." But what if the customer doesn't want to use it? What if they don't like using it? From a design thinking point of view, it is clear that "working" isn't sufficient. Instead, we need to deliver something that is consumable:

- **It works.** What we produce must be functional and provide the outcomes that our stakeholders expect.
- **It's usable.** Our solution should work well, with a well-designed user experience (UX).
- **It's desirable.** People should want to work with our solution, and better yet, feel a need to work with it, and where appropriate, pay us for it. As the first principle of Disciplined Agile recommends, our solution should delight our customers, not just satisfy them.

Additionally, what we produce isn't just software, but instead is a full-fledged solution that may include improvements to:

- **Software.** Software is an important part, but just a part, of our overall solution.
- **Hardware.** Our solutions run on hardware, and sometimes we need to evolve or improve that hardware.
- **Business processes.** We often improve the business processes around the usage of the system that we produce.
- **Organizational structure.** Sometimes the organization structure of the end users of our systems evolves to reflect changes in the functionality supported by it.
- **Supporting documentation.** Deliverable documentation, such as technical overviews and user manuals/help, is often a key aspect of our solutions.

DAD Terminology

Table 3.1 maps common DAD terms to the equivalent terms in other approaches. There are several important observations that we'd like to make about the terminology:

1. **There is no standard agile terminology.** There isn't an ISO industry standard for agile and, even if there was, it very likely would be ignored by agile practitioners.
2. **Scrum terminology is questionable at best.** When Scrum was first developed in the 1990s, its creators purposefully decided to choose unusual terminology, some adopted from the game of rugby, to indicate to people that it was different. That's perfectly fine, but given that DA is a hybrid we cannot limit it to apply arbitrary terms.
3. **Terms are important.** We believe terms should be clear. You need to explain what a scrum meeting is, and that it isn't a status meeting, whereas it's pretty clear what a coordination meeting is. Nobody sprints through a marathon.
4. **Choose whatever terms you like.** Having said all this, DAD doesn't prescribe terminology, so if you want to use terms like sprint, scrum meeting, or scrum master, then go ahead.
5. **Some mappings are tenuous.** An important thing to point out is that the terms don't map perfectly. For example, we know that there are differences between coaches, scrum masters, and project managers, but those differences aren't pertinent for this discussion.

Table 3.1: Mapping Some of the Varying Terminology in the Agile Community

DAD	Scrum	Spotify	XP	SAFe®	Traditional
Architecture owner	-	-	Coach	Solution architect	Solution architect
Coordination meeting	Daily standup	Huddle	-	Daily standup	Status meeting
Domain expert	-	Customer	Customer	Product owner	Subject matter expert (SME)
Iteration	Sprint	Sprint	Iteration	Iteration	Timebox
Product owner	Product owner	Product owner	Customer representative	Product owner	Change control board (CCB)
Stakeholder	-	Customer	Customer	Customer	Stakeholder
Team	Team	Squad, tribe	Team	Team	Team
Team lead	Scrum master	Agile coach	Coach	Scrum master	Project manager

Context Counts: DAD Provides the Foundation for Scaling Agile Tactically

Disciplined Agile (DA) distinguishes between two types of "agility at scale":

1. **Tactical agility at scale.** This is the application of agile and lean strategies on individual DAD teams. The goal is to apply agile deeply to address all of the complexities, what we call scaling factors, appropriately.
2. **Strategic agility at scale.** This is the application of agile and lean strategies broadly across your entire organization. This includes all divisions and teams within your organization, not just your software development teams.

Let's examine what it means to tactically scale agile solution delivery. When many people hear "scaling," they often think about large teams that may be geographically distributed in some way. This clearly happens, and people are clearly succeeding at applying agile in these sorts of situations, but there's often more to scaling than this. Organizations are also applying agile in compliance situations, either regulatory compliance that is imposed upon them, such as the Health Insurance Portability and Accountability Act (HIPAA); Personal Information Protection and Electronic Documents Act (PIPEDA); or General Data Protection Regulation (GDPR), or self-selected compliance, such as Capability Maturity Model Integration (CMMI) [CMMI]; International Organization for Standardization (ISO); and Information Technology Infrastructure Library (ITIL). They are also applying agile to a range of domain and technical complexities, even when multiple organizations are involved (as in outsourcing). Figure 3.6 summarizes the potential tactical scaling factors that you need to consider when tailoring your agile strategy. These scaling factors are a subset of the factors described in the Situation Context Framework (SCF) in Chapter 2 [SCF]. The further out on each scale you are, the greater the risk that you face.

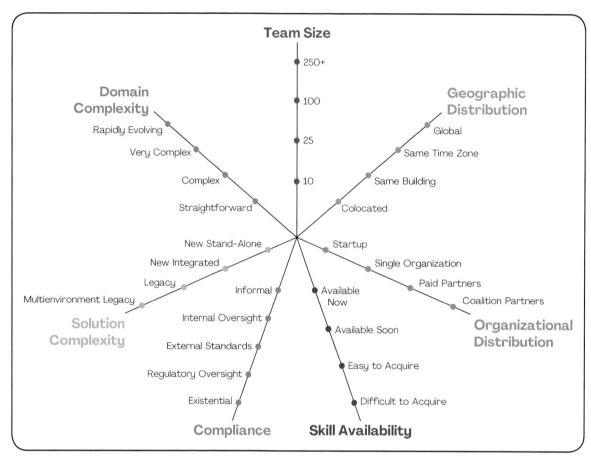

Figure 3.6 Tactical scaling factors.

DAD provides a solid foundation for tactically scaling agile in several ways:

- DAD promotes a risk-value life cycle where teams attack the riskier work early to help eliminate some or all of the risk, thereby increasing the chance of success. Some people like to refer to this as an aspect of "failing fast," although we like to put it in terms of learning fast or, better yet, succeeding early.
- DAD promotes self-organization enhanced with effective governance based on the observation that agile teams work within the scope and constraints of a larger organizational ecosystem. As a result, DAD recommends that you adopt an effective governance strategy that guides and enables agile teams.
- DAD promotes the delivery of consumable solutions over just the construction of working software.
- DAD promotes enterprise awareness over team awareness (this is a fundamental principle of DA, as discussed in Chapter 2). What we mean by this is that the team should do what's right for the organization—work to a common vision, leverage existing legacy systems and data sources, and follow common guidelines—and not just do what's convenient or fun for them.
- DAD is context-sensitive and goal-driven, not prescriptive (another DA principle is that choice is good). One process approach does not fit all, and DAD teams have the autonomy to choose and evolve their WoW.

It's Easy to Get Started With DAD

We'd like to share several strategies that we've seen applied to get people, teams, and organizations started with DAD:

1. **Read this book.** A good way for individuals to get started is to read this book.
2. **Take training.** Even after reading this book, you're likely to benefit from training as it will help to round out your knowledge. At some point we hope that you choose to pursue a Disciplined Agile certification.
3. **Start with a prescribed method/framework, then work your way out of "method prison."** Teams might choose to start with an existing method, such as Scrum or SAFe, and then apply the strategies described in this book to evolve their WoW from there.
4. **Start with DAD.** We believe that it's easier to start with DAD to begin with and thereby avoid running into the limitations of prescriptive methods.
5. **Work with an experienced agile coach.** We highly suggest you bring in a Disciplined Agile Coach (DAC)™ to help guide you through applying the DA tool kit.

Organizational adoption of Disciplined Agile will take time, potentially years when you decide to support agile WoWs across all aspects of your organization. Agile transformations such as this, which evolve into continuous improvement efforts at the organizational level, are the topics of Chapters 7 and 8 in our book, *An Executive's Guide to Disciplined Agile* [AmblerLines2017].

In Summary

Disciplined Agile Delivery (DAD) provides a pragmatic approach for addressing the unique situations in which solution delivery teams find themselves. DAD explicitly addresses the issues faced by enterprise agile teams that many agile methodologies prefer to gloss over. This includes how to successfully initiate agile teams in a streamlined manner, how architecture fits into the agile life cycle, how to address documentation effectively, how to address quality issues in an enterprise environment, how agile analysis techniques are applied to address the myriad of stakeholder concerns, how to govern agile and lean teams, and many more critical issues.

In this chapter, you learned that:

- DAD is the delivery portion of Disciplined Agile (DA).
- If you are using Scrum, XP, or Kanban, you are already using variations of a subset of DAD.
- You can start with your existing WoW and then apply DAD to improve it gradually. You don't need to make a risky "big bang" change.
- DAD provides six life cycles to choose from; it doesn't prescribe a single approach, providing you with solid choices on which to base your WoW.
- DAD addresses key enterprise concerns and shows how to do so in a context-sensitive manner.
- DAD does the heavy process lifting so that you don't have to.
- DAD shows how agile development works from beginning to end.
- DAD provides a flexible foundation from which to tactically scale mainstream methods.
- It is easy to get started with DAD, and there are multiple paths to do so.

Chapter 4

Roles, Rights, and Responsibilities

Alone we can do so little, together we can do so much. –Helen Keller

---

Key Points in This Chapter

- DAD suggests there are five primary roles: team lead, product owner, team member, architecture owner, and stakeholder.
- An architecture owner is the technical leader of the team and represents the architecture interests of the organization.
- DAD's stakeholder role recognizes that we need to delight all stakeholders, not just our customers.
- In many situations, teams will rely on people in supporting roles—specialists, domain experts, technical experts, independent testers, or integrators—as appropriate and as needed.
- DAD's roles are meant to be, like everything else, a suggested starting point. You may have valid reasons for tailoring the roles in your organization.

This chapter explores the potential rights and responsibilities of people involved with Disciplined Agile Delivery (DAD) teams, and the roles that they may choose to take on [DADRoles]. We say potential because you may discover that you need to tailor these ideas to fit into your organization's cultural environment. However, our experience is that the further you stray from the advice we provide below, the greater the risk you will take on. As always, do the best you can do in the situation that you face and strive to improve over time. Let's start with general rights and responsibilities.

Rights and Responsibilities

Becoming agile requires a culture change within your organization, and all cultures have rules, some explicit and some implicit, so that everyone understands their expected behavior. One way to define expected behavior is to negotiate the rights and responsibilities that people have. Interestingly, a lot of very good thinking on this topic was done in the Extreme Programming (XP) method, ideas which we've evolved for Disciplined Agile (DA) [RightsResponsibilities]. The following lists of potential rights and responsibilities are meant to act as a potential starting point for your team.

As agile team members, we have the right to:

- Be treated with respect.
- Work in a "safe environment."
- Produce and receive quality work based upon agreed-upon standards.
- Choose and evolve our way of working (WoW).

- Self-organize and plan our work, signing up for tasks that we will work on.
- Own the estimation process—the people who do the work are the ones who estimate the work.
- Determine how the team will work together—the people who do the work are the ones who plan the work.
- Be provided good-faith information and decisions in a timely manner.

To misquote Uncle Ben Parker, with great rights come great responsibilities. Agile team members have the responsibility to:

- Optimize our WoW.
- Be willing to collaborate extensively within our team.
- Share all information, including "work in process."
- Coach others in our skills and experience.
- Expand our knowledge and skills outside our specialty.
- Validate our work as early as possible, working with others to do so.
- Attend coordination meetings in person or through other means if not colocated.
- Proactively look for ways to improve team performance.
- For teams following an Agile life cycle (see Chapter 6), avoid accepting work outside of the current iteration without consent from the team.
- Make all work visible at all times, typically via a task board, so that current team work and capacity are transparent.

Potential Roles

DAD provides a set of five primary roles "out of the box," three of which are similar to those of Scrum. As you see in Figure 4.1, DAD has a team lead (such as a senior scrum master or project manager), product owner, and team member. DAD adds stakeholder (an extension of customer) and a role that we have seen to be extremely valuable in enterprise settings, that of architecture owner. Ideally, we have a "whole team," wherein we have all the skills on the team required to get the job done. However, while not ideal, in nontrivial situations it is common to require skills from outside the team and, as such, DAD includes a set of supporting roles that may join the team as needed.

To start, let's explore the primary roles.

Stakeholder

A stakeholder is someone who is materially impacted by the outcome of the solution. In this regard, the stakeholder is clearly more than an end user or customer. A stakeholder could be a:

- Direct user;
- Indirect user;
- Manager of users;
- Senior leader;
- Operations staff member;
- The "gold owner" who funds the team;
- Support (help desk) staff member;
- Auditor;

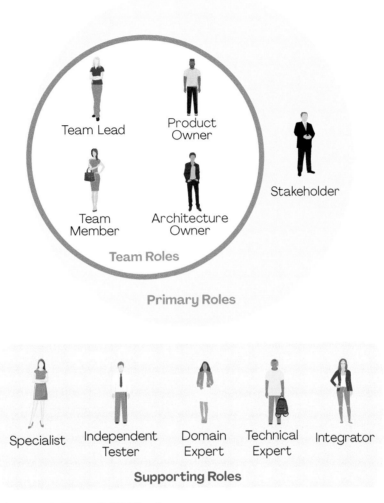

Figure 4.1 Potential DAD roles.

- Program/portfolio manager;
- Developer working on other solutions that integrate or interact with ours;
- Maintenance professional potentially affected by the development and/or deployment of a software-based solution; or
- Many more roles.

Product Owner

The product owner (PO) is the person on the team who speaks as the "one voice of the stakeholder" [ScrumGuide]. As you see in Figure 4.2, they represent the needs and desires of the stakeholder community to the agile delivery team. As such, the product owner clarifies any details regarding stakeholder desires or requirements for the solution and is also responsible for prioritizing the work that the team performs to deliver the solution. While the product owner may not be able to answer all questions, it is their responsibility to track down the answer in a timely manner so that the team can stay focused on their tasks.

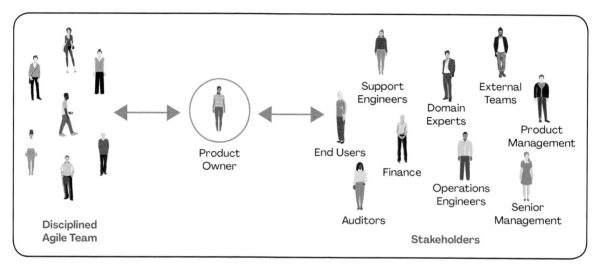

Figure 4.2 The product owner as a bridge between the team and stakeholders.

Each DAD team, or subteam in the case of large programs organized as a team of teams, has a single product owner. A secondary goal for a product owner is to represent the work of the agile team to the stakeholder community. This includes arranging demonstrations of the solution as it evolves and communicating team status to key stakeholders.

As a stakeholder proxy, the product owner:

- Is the "go-to" person for domain information;
- Provides information and makes decisions in a timely manner;
- Prioritizes all work for the team, including but not limited to requirements (perhaps captured as user stories), defects to be fixed, technical debt to be paid down, and more (The product owner takes both stakeholder and team needs into account when doing so.);
- Continually reprioritizes and adjusts scope based on evolving stakeholder needs;
- Is an active participant in modeling and acceptance testing;
- Helps the team gain access to expert stakeholders;
- Accepts the work of the team as either done or not done;
- Facilitates requirements modeling sessions, including requirements envisioning and look-ahead modeling;
- Educates the team in the business domain; and
- Is the gateway to funding.

When representing the agile team to the stakeholder community, the product owner:

- Is the public face of the team to stakeholders;
- Demos the solution to key stakeholders, which may include coaching team members to run the demo;
- Announces releases;
- Monitors and communicates team status to interested stakeholders, which may include educating stakeholders on how to access and understand the team's automated dashboard;

- Organizes milestone reviews, which should be kept as simple as possible (covered in the Govern Team process goal);
- Educates stakeholders in the delivery team's way of working (WoW); and
- Negotiates priorities, scope, funding, and schedules.

It is important to note that product owner tends to be a full-time job, and may even require help at scale in complex domains. A common challenge that we see in organizations new to agile is that they try to staff this role with someone on a part-time basis, basically tacking the product owner role onto an already busy person.

Team Member

Team members focus on producing the solution for stakeholders. Team members will perform testing, analysis, architecture, design, programming, planning, estimation, and many more activities as appropriate. Note that not every team member will have every single one of these skills, at least not yet, but they will have a subset of them and they will strive to gain more skills over time. Ideally, team members are generalizing specialists, someone with one or more specialties (such as analysis, programming, testing, etc.), a general knowledge of the delivery process, at least a general knowledge of the domain that they're working in, and the willingness to pick up new skills and knowledge from others [GenSpec]. Figure 4.3 compares four categories of skill levels: specialists who are narrowly focused on a single specialty, generalists with a broad knowledge who are often good at organizing and coordinating others but who do not have the detailed skills required to do the work, experts who have deep knowledge and skills in many specialties, and generalizing specialists who are a happy medium between generalists and specialists.

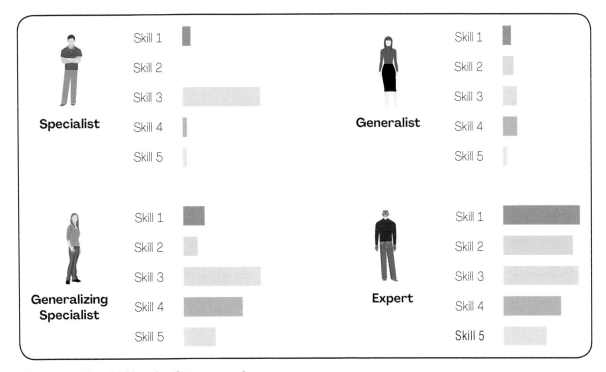

Figure 4.3 The skill levels of team members.

In practice, requiring people to be generalizing specialists can be daunting at first, particularly for people who are new to agile, because this is very different than the traditional approach of having generalists manage teams of specialists. The traditional approach is problematic because of the overhead required to make it work—specialists do their jobs, producing something for the next group of specialists downstream from them. To move the work along, they need to write and maintain documentation, often containing new versions of information that has already been documented upstream from them in the process. In short, specialists inject a lot of waste into the process with interim artifacts, reviews of these artifacts, and wait time to do the reviews. Generalizing specialists, on the other hand, have a wider range of skills enabling them to collaborate more effectively with others, to do a wider range of work and thereby avoid creation of interim artifacts. They work smarter, not harder.

The challenge is that if you're new to agile, then you very likely have staff who are either generalists or specialists, but very few generalizing specialists. The implication is that if you currently have people who are either specialists or generalists, then you put your teams together with these people. Because you want to improve your team's productivity, you help your team members become generalizing specialists through nonsolo work techniques such as pair programming, mob programming, and modeling with others (covered in the Grow Team Members process goal). By doing so, over several months specialists will pick up a wider range of skills and become more effective generalizing specialists as a result.

In addition to the general rights and responsibilities described earlier, team members have several additional responsibilities. They will:

- **Self-organize.** Team members will identify tasks, estimate tasks, sign up for tasks, perform the tasks, and track their status toward completion.
- **Go to the product owner (PO) for domain information and decisions.** Although team members will provide input to the product owner, in the end the product owner is responsible for providing the requirements and prioritizing the work, not the team members. It requires significant discipline on the part of team members to respect this, and to not add new features (known as "scope creep") or to guess at the details.
- **Work with the architecture owner (AO) to evolve the architecture.** The architecture owner is responsible for guiding the team through architecture and design work. Team members will work closely and collaboratively with the architecture owner to identify and evolve the architectural strategy. When the team is unable to come to an agreement around the direction to take, the architecture owner may need to be the tie breaker and choose what they feel to be the best option, which team members are expected to support. More on this below.
- **Follow enterprise conventions and leverage and enhance the existing infrastructure.** One of the DA principles (see Chapter 2) is to be enterprise aware. An implication of this is that DAD team members will adopt and have the discipline to tailor, where appropriate, any enterprise/corporate coding standards, user interface design conventions, database guidelines, and so on. They should also try to reuse and enhance existing, reusable assets such as common web services, frameworks, and yes, even existing legacy data sources. DAD includes the Leverage and Enhance Existing Infrastructure process goal to specifically address this strategy.
- **Lead meetings.** Although other agile methods will assign this responsibility to the team lead, the fact is that anyone on the team can lead or facilitate meetings. The team lead is merely responsible for ensuring that this happens.

Why not call a team lead a scrum master?

Since DA supports several life cycle approaches, not every team in your organization is likely to use Scrum. An agile team might be led by a senior scrum master, a project team by a project manager, a lean software team by a tech lead, a sales team by a sales manager, and so on. Different types of teams will have different types of team leads.

Team Lead

An important aspect of self-organizing teams is that team leads facilitate or guide the team in performing technical management activities instead of taking on these responsibilities themselves. The team lead is a servant leader to the team, or better yet a host leader [Host], creating and maintaining the conditions that allow the team to be successful. This can be a hard role to fill—attitude is key to their success. Team lead is typically a role, not a title. Depending on the type of team, a team lead may have the title of senior scrum master for an agile product team, scrum master for a simple scrum team, project manager for an agile project team, marketing director for a marketing team, chief enterprise architect for an enterprise architecture team, and so on. Different types of teams will have different types of team leads and, very likely, different job titles.

On high-performance teams, the team lead role will often rotate within the team if they are comfortable doing that. On these teams, leadership is shared, spreading the burden (and monotony) of ceremony facilitation across several people.

The team lead is also an agile coach, or perhaps a "junior agile coach" is more accurate, given that a Disciplined Agile Coach (DAC)™ typically works with several, and often disparate teams, whereas a team lead focuses on coaching their team. As a coach, the team lead helps to keep the team focused on delivering work items and fulfilling the iteration goals and commitments that they have made to the product owner. They act as a true leader, facilitating communication, empowering them to choose their way of working (WoW), ensuring that the team has the resources that it needs, and removing any impediments to the team (issue resolution) in a timely manner. When teams are self-organizing, effective leadership is crucial to their success.

Notice how we said that the team lead coaches, rather than owns or dictates, the team's WoW. In DA, the entire team is responsible for their WoW, not just team leadership or, worse yet, someone outside of the team.

A team lead's leadership responsibilities can be summarized as:

- Guides the team through choosing and evolving their WoW;
- Facilitates close collaboration across all roles and functions;
- Ensures that the team is fully functional and productive;
- Keeps the team focused within the context of their vision and goals;
- Is responsible for removal of team-based impediments and for the escalation of organization-wide impediments, collaborating with organizational leadership to do so;

- Protects the team from interruptions and external interferences;
- Maintains open, honest communication between everyone involved;
- Coaches others in the use and application of agile practices;
- Prompts the team to discuss and think through issues when they're identified;
- Facilitates decision-making, but does not make decisions or mandate internal team activity; and
- Ensures that the team keeps their focus on producing a potentially consumable solution.

When a team lead is leading a project team or functional team (such as a marketing team), the team lead may be asked to take on the management responsibilities that agile frameworks often downplay. The optional responsibilities that a team lead may be required to fulfill, and the challenges associated in doing so, include:

- **Assessing team members.** There are several strategies for assessing or providing feedback to people, described by the Grow Team Members process goal, that you may apply. Doing so is often the responsibility of a resource manager, but sometimes people in these roles are not available. When a team lead is responsible for assessing their fellow team members, it puts them in a position of authority over the people they're supposed to lead and collaborate with. This in turn can significantly alter the dynamics of the relationship that team members have with the team lead, reducing their psychological safety when working with the team lead because they don't know how doing so will affect their assessment.
- **Managing the team's budget.** Although the product owner is typically the gateway to funding, somebody may be required to track and report how the funds are spent. If the product owner does not do this then the team lead typically becomes responsible for doing so.
- **Management reporting.** This ensures that someone on the team (perhaps themselves) captures relevant team metrics and reports team progress to organizational leadership. Hopefully this type of reporting is automated via dashboard technology, but if not, the team lead is often responsible for manually generating any required reports. The Organize Metrics and Measure Outcomes process goals address metrics in detail.
- **Obtains resources.** The team lead is often responsible for ensuring that collaborative tools, such as task boards for team coordination and whiteboards for modeling, are available to the team.
- **Meeting facilitation.** This ensures that someone on the team (sometimes themselves) facilitates the various meetings (coordination meetings, iteration planning meetings, demos, modeling sessions, and retrospectives).

The team lead role is often a part-time effort, particularly on smaller teams. The implication is that a team lead either needs to have the skills to also be a team member, or perhaps in some cases an architecture owner (more on this below). However, on a team new to agile the coaching aspects of being a team lead are critical to your success at adopting agile. This is something that organizations new to agile can struggle with conceptually because they've never had to make a similar investment in their staff's growth.

Another alternative is to have someone be the team lead on two or three teams, although that requires the teams to stagger their ceremonies such as coordination meetings, demos, and retrospectives so that the team lead can be involved. This can work with teams that are experienced with agile thinking and techniques because they don't require as much coaching. Furthermore, as teams gel and become adept at self-organization, there is less need for someone to be in the team lead role and it may be sufficient for someone to step up from time to time to address team lead responsibilities.

Architecture Owner

The architecture owner (AO) is the person who guides the team through architecture and design decisions, facilitating the identification and evolution of the overall solution design [AgileModeling]. On small teams, the person in the role of team lead will often also be in the role of architecture owner, assuming they have the skills for both roles. Having said that, our experience is that it is hard enough to find someone qualified to fill either of these roles, let alone both.

Although the architecture owner is typically the senior developer on the team—and sometimes may be known as the technical architect, software architect, or solution architect—it should be noted that this is not a hierarchical position into which other team members report. They are expected to sign up and deliver work related to tasks just like any other team member. Architecture owners should have a technical background and a solid understanding of the business domain.

The responsibilities of the architecture owner include:

- Guiding the creation and evolution of the architecture of the solution that the team is working on (Note that the architecture owner is not solely responsible for the architecture; instead, they lead the architecture and design discussions.);
- Mentoring and coaching other team members in architecture practices and issues;
- Understanding the architectural direction and standards of your organization and helping to ensure that the team adheres to them appropriately;
- Working closely with enterprise architects, if they exist, or they may even be an enterprise architect (Note that this can be an interesting change for larger organizations where their enterprise architects are not currently actively involved with teams. This is quite common for smaller organizations.);
- Working closely with the product owner to help them to understand the needs of technical stakeholders, the implications of technical debt, and the need to invest in paying it down, and in some cases to understand and interact with team members more effectively;
- Understanding existing enterprise assets such as frameworks, patterns, and subsystems, and ensuring that the team uses them where appropriate;
- Ensuring that the solution will be easy to support by encouraging good design and refactoring to minimize technical debt (the focus of DAD's Improve Quality process goal);
- Ensuring that the solution is integrated and tested on a regular basis, ideally via a continuous integration (CI) strategy;
- Having the final say regarding technical decisions, but trying to avoid dictating the architectural direction in favor of a collaborative, team-based approach (The architecture owner should work very closely with the team to identify and determine strategies to mitigate key technical risks, addressed by DAD's Prove Architecture Early process goal.); and
- Leading the initial architecture-envisioning effort at the beginning of a release and supporting the initial requirements-envisioning effort (particularly when it comes to understanding and evolving the nonfunctional requirements for the solution).

Potential Supporting Roles

We would like to be able to say that all you need are the five primary roles described above to succeed. The fact is the primary roles don't cover the entire gamut—it's unlikely your team will have all of the technical expertise that it needs. Your product owner couldn't possibly have expert knowledge in all aspects of the domain, and even if your organization had experts at all aspects of solution delivery, it couldn't possibly staff every single team with the full range of expertise required. Your team may have the need to add some or all of the following roles:

1. **Domain expert (subject matter expert).** The product owner represents a wide range of stakeholders, not just end users, so it isn't reasonable to expect them to be experts in every nuance of the domain, something that is particularly true in complex domains. The product owner will sometimes bring in domain experts to work with the team (e.g., a tax expert to explain the details of a requirement or the sponsoring executive to explain the vision).
2. **Specialist.** Although most agile team members are generalizing specialists, sometimes, particularly at scale, specialists are required. For example, on large teams or in complex domains one or more agile business analysts may join the team to help explore the requirements for what you're building. On very large teams, a program manager may be required to coordinate the team leads on various squads/subteams. You will also see specialists on teams when generalizing specialists aren't yet available—when your organization is new to agile it may be staffed with specialists who haven't yet made the transition to generalizing specialists.
3. **Technical expert.** Sometimes the team needs the help of technical experts, such as a build master to set up their build scripts, an agile database administrator to help design and test their database, or a security expert to provide advice around writing a secure solution. Technical experts are brought in on an as-needed, temporary basis to help the team overcome a difficult problem and to transfer their skills to one or more developers on the team. Technical experts are often working on other teams that are responsible for enterprise-level technical concerns or are simply specialists on loan to your team from other delivery teams.
4. **Independent tester.** Although the majority of the testing is done by the people on the DAD team themselves, some teams are supported by an independent test team working in parallel that will validate their work throughout the life cycle. This independent test team is typically needed for scaling situations within complex domains, using complex technology, or addressing regulatory compliance issues.
5. **Integrator.** For large DAD teams that have been organized into a team of subteams/squads, the subteams are typically responsible for one or more subsystems or features. Generally, the larger the overall team, the larger and more complicated the solution being built. In these situations, the overall team may require one or more people in the role of integrator responsible for building the entire solution from its various subsystems. On smaller teams or in simpler situations, the architecture owner is typically responsible for ensuring integration, a responsibility that is picked up by the integrator(s) for more complex environments. Integrators often work closely with the independent test team, if there is one, to perform system integration testing regularly throughout the release. This integrator role is typically only needed at scale for complex technical solutions.

An interesting implication for organizations that are new to agile is that the agile teams may need access to people in these supporting roles earlier in the life cycle than they are accustomed to with traditional teams. And the timing of the access is often a bit less predictable, due to the evolutionary nature of agile, than with traditional development. We've found that people in these supporting roles will need to be flexible.

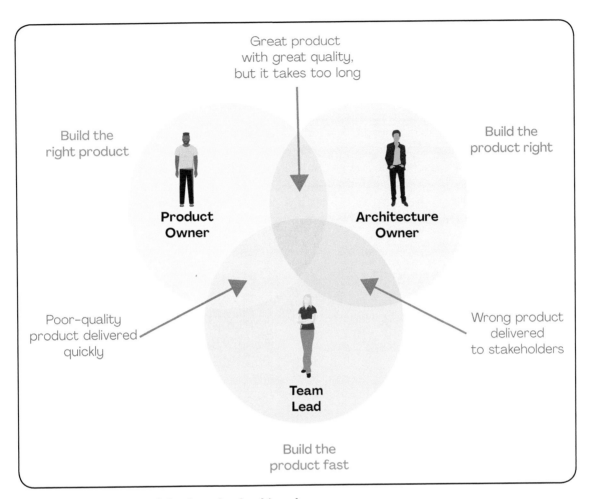

Figure 4.4 Viewpoints of the three leadership roles.

The Three Leadership Roles

We often refer to the team lead, product owner, and architecture owner as the leadership triumvirate of the team. As you see in Figure 4.4, the product owner is focused on getting the right product built, the architecture owner on building the product right, and the team lead on building it fast. All three of these priorities must be balanced through close collaboration by the people in these roles. Figure 4.4 also indicates what happens when one of these priorities is ignored. When teams are new to agile, the center spot may prove to be quite small at first, but over time the people in these three leadership roles, and more importantly the entire team itself, will help to grow it.

Do We Need the Scrum Roles at All?

In the 1990s when Scrum was created, it was a different world. We were used to working in specialist silos, building software from documents, and didn't really know how and when to collaborate, hence the need for a scrum master to forcibly bring team members together, unifying them behind a team goal. These days, many younger developers have never worked in a siloed environment. They don't need a designated role within the team to ensure collaboration happens effectively. Similarly, why do we need a formal product owner between the team and the rest of our stakeholders?

This degree of separation increases the chances of miscommunications and limits opportunities of the teams to develop empathy for the people they are building the solution for. In Scrum's early days, it was difficult to gain access to stakeholders so the "mandatory" product owner was created. It is more commonly accepted practice these days to have direct access to all stakeholders, and hopefully active stakeholder participation.

In Disciplined Agile, we constantly need to remind teams that context counts and choice is good. Like everything in DA, the roles we outline are "good ideas" which may or may not make sense for you. In the Form Team process goal, we encourage you to consider the roles that make sense for your team. If you are new to agile and there is little organizational resistance to change, then you probably want to adopt the classic DAD roles. If your agile maturity and capability are more advanced, or if adopting new roles would be too disruptive, then you may wish to adapt roles accordingly.

Tailoring DAD Team Roles for Your Organization

As we mentioned earlier, you build your teams from the people that you have. Many organizations find that they cannot staff some of the roles, or that some of the DAD roles simply don't fit well in their existing culture. As a result, they find they need to tailor the roles to reflect the situation that they find themselves in. Tailoring the roles can be a very slippery slope as we've found the DAD roles work very well in practice, so any tailoring that you do likely increases the risk faced by the team. Table 4.1 captures tailoring options for the primary roles, and the risks associated with doing so.

DAD and Traditional Roles

Many agile purists will insist that traditional roles such as project manager, business analyst (BA), resource manager, and many others go away with agile. Although that *may* happen in the long run, it isn't practical in the short term. The elimination of traditional roles at the beginning of your agile transformation is revolutionary and often results in resistance to, and the undermining of, agile adoption. We prefer a more evolutionary, less disruptive approach that respects people and their career aspirations. While agile requires different ways of working, the skills and rigor of traditional specialties are still extremely valuable. Project managers understand risk management, estimating strategies, and release planning. Classically trained or certified business analysts bring a rich tool kit of modeling options (many of which are described in the Explore Scope goal). To say that we don't need project managers or business analysts is short-sighted, naïve, and disrespectful to these professions.

Having said that, the primary DAD roles are extremely effective in practice. When we work with organizations to improve their WoW, we help as many people as we can to transition out of their existing traditional roles into the DAD roles, which they often find more fulfilling in practice. Figure 4.5 depicts common options for several traditional roles. What we show are generalizations, and it's important to recognize that people will choose their own career paths based on their own preferences and desires—everyone has career options in agile. The important thing is to recognize that everyone can find a place for themselves in an agile organization if they're willing to learn a new WoW and move into new roles.

Table 4.1 Potential Tailoring Options for the Primary Roles

Role	Tailoring Options and Risks
Architecture owner	• **Application/solution architect.** A traditional architect does not work as collaboratively as an architecture owner, so runs the risk of having their vision misunderstood or ignored by the team. • **No architecture owner.** Without someone in the architecture owner role, the team must actively collaborate to identify an architectural strategy on their own, which tends to lead to the team missing architectural concerns and paying the price later in the life cycle with increased rework.
Product owner	• **Business analyst.** Business analysts typically don't have the decision-making authority that a product owner does, so they become a bottleneck when the team needs a decision quickly. Business analysts also tend to favor production of requirements documentation rather than direct collaboration with team members. • **Active stakeholder participation.** Team members work directly with stakeholders to understand their needs and to gain feedback on their work. The team will need a way to identify and work to a consistent vision, otherwise they risk getting pulled in multiple directions.
Stakeholder	• **Personas.** Although there are always stakeholders, you might not have access to them, or more accurately, access to the full range of them. Personas are fictional characters that represent classes of stakeholders. Personas enable the team to talk in terms of these fictional people and to explore how these people would interact with the solution.
Team lead	• **Scrum master.** We've had mixed results with scrum masters on teams, mostly because the Certified ScrumMaster® (CSM) designation requires very little effort to gain. As a result, we suggest that you put a qualified senior scrum master into this role, not just a CSM. • **Project manager.** By assigning work to people and then monitoring them, a project manager will negate a team's ability to benefit from self-organization and will very likely decrease psychological safety on the team. Having said that, a significant percentage of project managers are willing, and able, to drop command-and-control strategies in favor of a leadership approach. • **No team lead.** We have seen teams that are truly self-organizing that do not need a team lead. There have always been teams that have been working together for a long time where people choose to address what would normally be team lead responsibilities as needed, just like any other type of work.
Team member	• **Specialists.** As we said earlier, if all you have available are specialists, then that's what you build your team from.

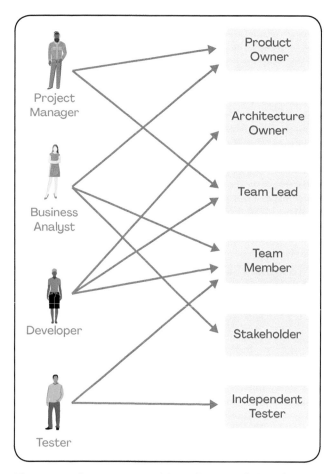

Figure 4.5 Common transitions from traditional to DAD roles.

In Summary

This chapter explored the potential rights and responsibilities of people involved with DAD teams, and the roles that they may choose to take on. We say potential because you need to tailor these ideas to fit into your organization's cultural environment. However, we showed that the further you stray from the DAD roles and responsibilities, the greater the risk you will take on. You learned:

- DAD defines five primary roles—team lead, product owner, team member, architecture owner, and stakeholder—that appear on all teams.
- In many situations, teams will rely on people in supporting roles—specialists, domain experts, technical experts, independent testers, or integrators—as appropriate and as needed.
- DAD's roles are meant to be, like everything else, a suggested starting point. You may have valid reasons for tailoring the roles for your organization.
- With roles, as with everything else, do the best you can do in the situation that you face and strive to improve over time.

Chapter 5

Process Goals

We must learn not just to accept differences between ourselves and our ideas, but to enthusiastically welcome and enjoy them. —Gene Roddenberry

---

Key Points in This Chapter

- Although every team works in a unique way, they still need to address the same process goals (process outcomes).
- Process goals guide you through what you need to think about and your potential options; they don't prescribe what to do.
- DAD process goals provide you with choices, each of which has trade-offs.
- Strive to do the best you can do right now in the situation that you face.
- The DAD process goals appear overly complicated at first, but ask yourself what you would remove.

Disciplined Agile Delivery (DAD) takes a straightforward approach to support teams in choosing their way of working (WoW). Process goals guide teams through the process-related decisions that they need to make to tailor agile strategies to address the context of the situation that they face [Goals]. Some people like to call this capability-driven WoW, process outcomes-driven WoW, or a vector-driven approach.

Each of DAD's process goals define a high-level process outcome, such as improving quality or exploring the initial scope, without prescribing how to do so. Instead, a process goal indicates the issues you need to consider, what we call decision points, and some potential options you may choose to adopt.

Process goals guide teams through the process-related decisions that they need to make to tailor and scale agile strategies to address the context of the situation that they face. This tailoring effort should take hours at most, not days, and DAD's straightforward goal diagrams help you to streamline doing so. Process goals are a recommended approach to support teams in choosing their WoW, and are a critical part of the Disciplined Agile (DA) process scaffolding.

Why a Goal-Driven Approach?

In Chapter 1, we learned that there are several good reasons why a team should own their process and why they should choose and then evolve their WoW over time. First, every team faces a unique situation and therefore should tailor their approach to best address that situation and evolve their WoW as the situation evolves. In other words, context counts. Second, you need to have choices and know what those choices are—you can't own your process if you don't know what's for sale. Third, we want to be awesome at what we do, so we need the flexibility to experiment with ways of working so that we can discover how to be the most awesome team we can be.

Most teams struggle to truly own their process, mostly because they don't have the process expertise within the team to do so. So they need some help, and process goals are an important part of that help. Our experience is that there are several fundamental advantages to taking a goal-driven approach to agile solution delivery:

- It enables teams to focus on process outcomes, not on process compliance.
- It provides a concise, shared pathway to leaner, less wasteful process decisions.
- It supports choosing your WoW by making process decisions explicit.
- It makes your process options very clear and thereby makes it easier to identify the appropriate strategy for the situation you find yourself in.
- It enables effective scaling by providing you with strategies that are sophisticated enough to address the complexities that you face at scale.
- It takes the guesswork out of extending agile methods and thereby enables you to focus on your actual job, which is to provide value to your stakeholders.
- It makes it clear what risks you're taking on and thus enables you to increase the likelihood of success.
- It hints at an agile maturity model (this is important for any organization struggling to move away from traditional maturity models).

How Much Detail Is Enough?

The amount of process detail that you require as a person, or as a team, varies based on your situation. In general, the more experienced you are, the less detail you need. Figure 5.1 overviews how we've chosen to capture the details of DAD, starting with high-level, outcome-based process goals all the way down to the nitty-gritty details of a specific practice. The DA Browser [DABrowser] captures the first three levels: process goals, process goal diagrams, and option tables. The fourth level, detailed practice/strategy descriptions, would be tens of thousands of printed pages—the agile/lean canon is very, very large and our aim with DAD is to help put it in context for you.

As you see in Figure 5.1, there are four levels of detail when it comes to describing process goals:

1. **Process goal.** The named process outcome, for example: Identify Architecture Strategy, Accelerate Value Delivery, Deploy the Solution, or Grow Team Members. Named process goals are useful to provide a consistent language to discuss process-related issues across teams with potentially very different WoWs.
2. **Process goal diagram.** This is a visual depiction of the aspects you need to think through about the goal, what we call decision points, and several options for each decision point to choose from. We're not saying that we've identified every possible technique available to you, but we have identified enough to give you a good range of options and to make it clear that you do in fact have choices. In many ways, a process goal diagram is an advanced version of a decision tree, and an example of one is depicted in Figure 5.4 later in this chapter. Process goal diagrams

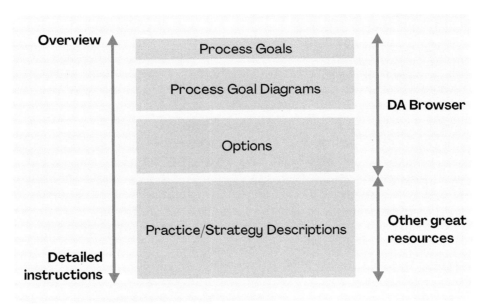

Figure 5.1 Level of details with process goals.

are useful for experienced practitioners, including agile coaches, as overviews of what they need to consider with tailoring the portion of their WoW addressed by that goal.

3. **Option tables.** An option table provides a brief summary of potential practices or strategies that you should consider adopting to address a given decision point. For each option the trade-offs associated with it are also provided so as to put it in context. There is no such thing as a best practice—every given practice/strategy works well in some contexts and is inappropriate in other contexts. Option tables help you to identify what you believe to be the best option for your team to experiment with in the current situation that you face. Figure 5.5 provides an example of one later in this chapter.

4. **Practice/strategy descriptions.** Every technique is described through blogs, articles, and in some cases, one or more books. For example, there are thousands of blog postings and articles about test-driven development (TDD), as well as several good books. Our aim is to point you in the right direction to these great resources, which is exactly what we do in the DA Browser.

Context Counts: Disciplined Agile Teams Are Goal-Driven

Figure 5.2 shows the goals for a DAD team grouped by the three phases of Inception, Construction, and Transition, as well as the goals that are ongoing throughout the life cycle.

If you know your process history, you may have noticed that we adopted the phase names from the Unified Process (UP) [Kruchten]. More accurately, we adopted three of the four names from UP because DAD doesn't have an elaboration phase, unlike UP. Some people will point to this as evidence that DAD is just UP, but if you're familiar with UP, you'll recognize that this clearly isn't true. We choose to adopt these names because, frankly, they were perfectly fine. Our philosophy is to reuse and leverage as many great ideas as possible, including terminology, and not invent new terminology if we can avoid doing so.

Process Goal Diagrams

Although listing the high-level process goals in Figure 5.2 is a good start, most people need more information than this. To go to the next level of detail we use goal diagrams, the notation for which is described in Figure 5.3 and an example of which is shown in Figure 5.4. First, let's explore the notation:

- **Process goals.** Process goals are shown as rounded rectangles.
- **Decision points.** Decision points, which are process issues that you need to consider addressing, are shown as rectangles. Process goals will have two or more decision points, with most goals having four or five decision points, although some have more. Each decision point can be addressed by practices/strategies that are presented in a list to the right. Sometimes there are decision points that you will not have to address given your situation. For example, the Coordinate Activities process goal has a Coordinate Across Program decision point that only applies if your team is part of a larger "team of teams."
- **Ordered option lists.** An ordered option list is depicted with an arrow to the left of the list of techniques. What we mean by this is that the techniques appearing at the top of the list are more desirable, generally more effective in practice, and the less desirable techniques are at the bottom of the list. Your team, of course, should strive to adopt the most effective techniques they are capable of performing given the context of the situation that they face. In other words, do the best that you can but be aware that there are potentially better techniques that you can choose to adopt at some point. From the point of view of complexity theory, a decision point with an ordered option list is effectively a vector that indicates a change path. In Figure 5.4, the Level of Detail of the Scope Document decision point has an ordered set of options whereas the second one does not.
- **Unordered option lists.** An unordered option list is depicted without an arrow—each option has advantages and disadvantages, but it isn't clear how to rank the options fairly.

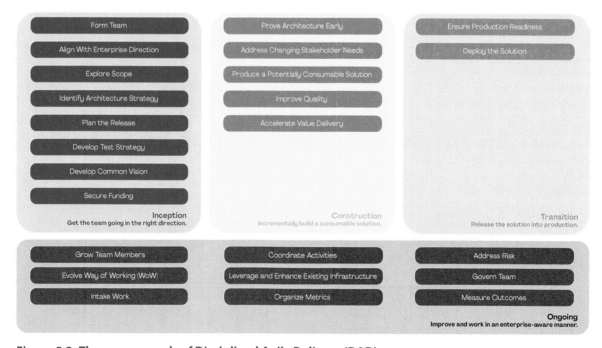

Figure 5.2 The process goals of Disciplined Agile Delivery (DAD).

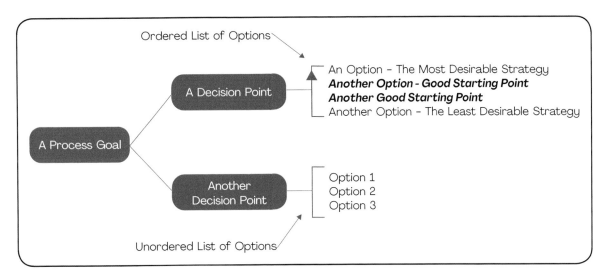

Figure 5.3 The notation of a process goal diagram.

- **Potential starting points.** Potential starting points are shown in bold italics. Because there may be many techniques to choose from, we indicate "default" techniques in bolded italics. These defaults are good starting points for small teams new to agile that are taking on a straightforward problem—they are almost always strategies from Scrum, Extreme Programming (XP), and Agile Modeling, with a few Unified Process ideas thrown in to round things out.

It is common to combine several options from a given list in practice. For example, consider the Explore Usage decision point in Figure 5.4—it is common for teams that are new to agile to apply epics, user stories, and user story maps to explore usage requirements.

Let's explore the Explore Scope goal diagram of Figure 5.4 a bit more. This is a process goal that you should address at the beginning of the life cycle during Inception (if you're following a life cycle that includes an Inception phase; see Chapter 6). Where some agile methods will simply advise you to initially populate a product backlog with some user stories, the goal diagram makes it clear that you might want to be a bit more sophisticated in your approach. What level of detail should you capture, if any? How are you going to explore potential usage of the system? Or the UI requirements? Or the business process(es) supported by the solution? Default techniques, or perhaps more accurately suggested starting points, are shown in bold italics. Notice how we suggest that you likely want to default to capturing usage in some way, basic domain concepts (e.g., via a high-level conceptual diagram) in some way, and nonfunctional requirements in some way. There are different strategies you may want to consider for modeling—choose the ones that make sense for your situation and not the ones that don't. You should also start thinking about your approach to managing your work—a light specification approach of writing up some index cards and a few whiteboard sketches is just one option you should consider. In DAD, we make it clear that agile teams do more than just implement new requirements, hence our recommendation to default to a work item list over a simplistic requirements (product) backlog strategy. Work items may include new requirements to be implemented, defects to be fixed, training workshops, reviews of other teams' work, and so on. These are all things that need to be sized, prioritized, and planned for. Finally, the goal diagram makes it clear that when you're exploring the initial scope of your effort that you should capture nonfunctional requirements—such as reliability, privacy, availability, performance, and security requirements (among many)—in some manner.

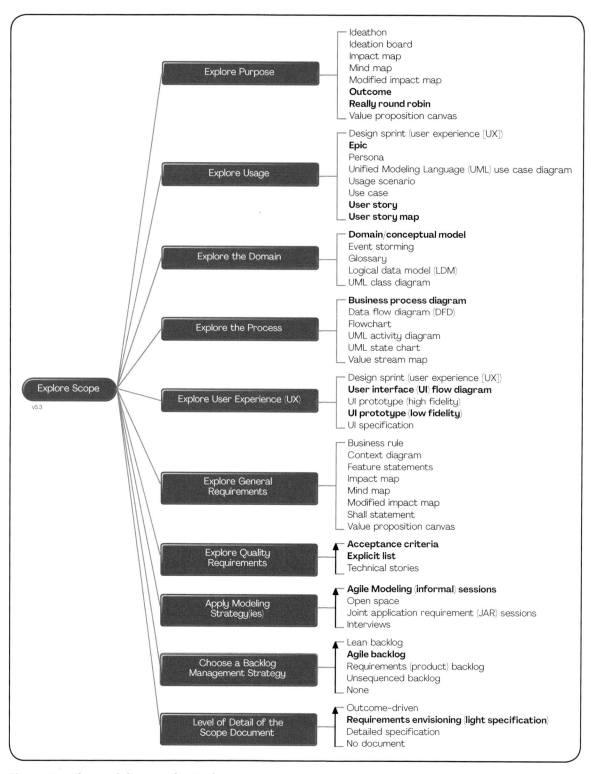

Figure 5.4 The goal diagram for Explore Scope.

But This Is So Complicated!

Our strategy with DA is to explicitly recognize that software development (and IT and organizations, in general) are inherently complicated. DA doesn't try to dumb things down into a handful of "best practices." Instead, DA explicitly communicates the issues that you face, the options that you have, and the trade-offs that you're making, and simplifies the process of choosing the right strategies that meet your needs. DA provides scaffolding to help you make better process decisions.

Yes, there are many process goals (24, in fact) depicted in Figure 5.2. Which would you take out? We've seen teams not address risk in any way, but that invariably went poorly for them. We've also seen teams choose not to address the goal Improve Quality, only to watch their technical debt rise. In practice, you can't safely choose to ignore any of these goals. Similarly, consider the decision points in Figure 5.4. Would you drop any of those? Likely not. Yes, it's daunting that there is so much to take into account to succeed at solution delivery in the long term, and what we've captured appears to be a minimal set for enterprise-class solution development.

Getting to the Details: Option Tables and References

The next level of detail is the option tables, an example of which is shown in Figure 5.5 for Explore Scope's Explore Quality Requirements decision point. Each table lists the options, which are practices or strategies, and the trade-offs of each one. The goal is to put each option into context and, where appropriate, point you to more detail about that technique.

In Figure 5.6, you can see how you are pointed to more information via links under the additional resources pull-down menu. In this case, you see links that are pertinent to the acceptance criteria option. These links lead to relevant articles, blog postings, books, or training opportunities. DA's philosophy is to provide sufficiently contextual information to determine whether an option is likely to work for you, and to point you to great resources if you want to learn more.

How to Apply Process Goals in Practice

Disciplined agilists can process goals in several common scenarios:

- **Identifying potential strategies to experiment with.** We described guided process improvement (GCI) in Chapter 1, where a team uses DAD as a reference to identify techniques to experiment with. Because DAD puts options into context, as you saw in Figure 5.5, you are more likely to identify a technique that will work for you in your environment.
- **Enhancing retrospectives.** The goal diagrams and supporting tables provide a tool kit of potential options that you can choose to experiment with to resolve challenges identified by the team.
- **Checklists.** Goal diagrams are often used by experienced teams to remind them of potential techniques that they could choose to apply in their current situation.
- **Process-tailoring workshops.** Described in Chapter 1, process-tailoring workshops are often used by new teams to identify or negotiate how they will work together. The process goals often prove to be great resources to help focus those workshops, and an easy way to use them is to print them out and put them up on the wall and then work through them as a team.

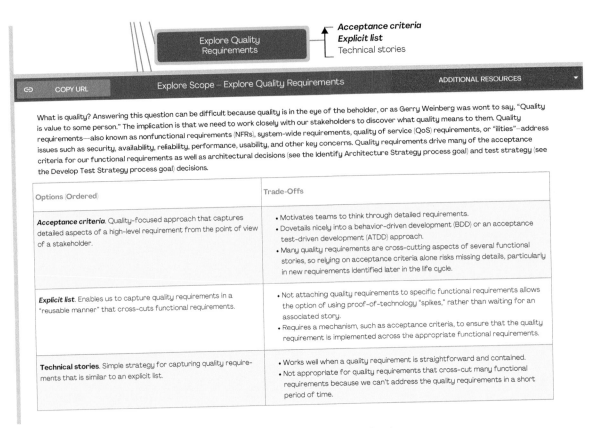

Figure 5.5 Explore Quality Requirements (DA Browser screen shot).

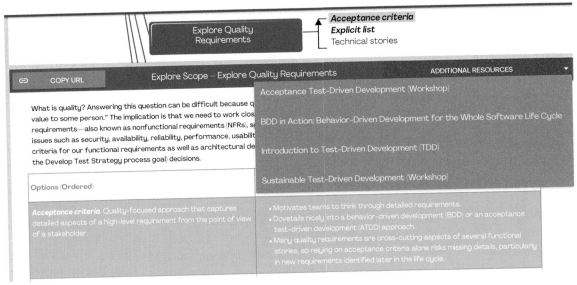

Figure 5.6 References for acceptance criteria (DA Browser screen shot).

- **Maturity model.**[1] The ordered decision points effectively provide a focused maturity model around a given decision point. More importantly, ordered decision points are effectively vectors indicating an improvement path for teams to potentially follow. This is similar to the CMMI Continuous Model strategy [CMMI].
- **Have productive discussions about process choices.** An interesting aspect of process goals is that some of the choices they provide really aren't very effective in practice. WHAT?! We sometimes find teams following a technique because they believe that's the best strategy available, maybe they've been told it's a "best practice," maybe it's the best strategy they know about, maybe it's the best they can do right now, or maybe it's been prescribed to them by their adopted methodology and they never thought to look beyond it. Regardless, this strategy plus other valid options are now provided to them, with the trade-offs for each clearly described. This puts you in a better position to compare and contrast strategies and potentially choose a new strategy to experiment with.

In Summary

This book describes how you can choose your WoW, and how your team can truly own its process. The only way you can own your process is if you know what's for sale. Process goals help to make your process choices, and the trade-offs associated with them, explicit. In this chapter, we explored several key concepts:

- Although every team works in a unique way, they still need to address the same process goals (process outcomes).
- Process goals guide you through what you need to think about and your potential options; they don't prescribe what to do.
- Process goals provide you with choices, each of which have trade-offs.
- Strive to do the best you can do right now in the situation that you face, and to learn and improve over time.
- If the process goals appear overly complicated at first, ask yourself what you would remove.

---

[1] In DA, we're not afraid to use "agile swear words" such as management, governance, phase, and yes, even "maturity model."

Chapter 6
Choosing the Right Life Cycle

May your choices reflect your hopes, not your fears. –Nelson Mandela

Key Points in This Chapter

- Some teams within your organization will still follow a traditional life cycle—DAD explicitly recognizes this but does not provide support for this shrinking category of work.
- DAD provides the scaffolding required for choosing between, and then evolving, six solution delivery life cycles (SDLCs) based on either agile or lean strategies.
- Project-based life cycles, even agile and lean ones, go through phases.
- Every life cycle has its advantages and disadvantages; each team needs to pick the one that best reflects their context.
- Common, lightweight, risk-based milestones enable consistent governance; you don't need to force teams to follow the same process.
- A team will start with a given life cycle and often evolve away from it as they continuously improve their WoW.

We have the privilege of working with organizations all over the world. When we go into an organization, often to coach them in how to improve their way of working (WoW), we get to observe what is actually happening within these organizations. One thing we see over and over again, in all but the very smallest of enterprises, is that they have several delivery life cycles in place across their teams. Some of these teams will be following a Scrum-based, agile project life cycle whereas others will have adopted a Kanban-based lean life cycle. The more advanced teams, particularly those moving toward a DevOps mindset, will have adopted a continuous delivery approach [Kim]. Some may be working on a brand-new business idea and are following an experimental "lean startup" style of approach, and some teams may still be following a more traditional life cycle. The reason why this happens, as we described in Chapter 2, is because each team is unique and in a unique situation. Teams need a WoW that reflects the context that they face, and an important part of choosing an effective WoW is to select a life cycle that best fits their situation. Disciplined Agile Delivery (DAD) scaffolding provides life cycle choices to your delivery teams, while enabling consistent governance across them [LifeCycles].

A Quick History Lesson: The Serial Life Cycle

First and foremost, the traditional life cycle is not currently supported by DAD. There are several different flavors of the serial life cycle, sometimes called the traditional life cycle, the waterfall life cycle, or even the predictive life cycle. Figure 6.1 depicts what is known as the V model. The basic

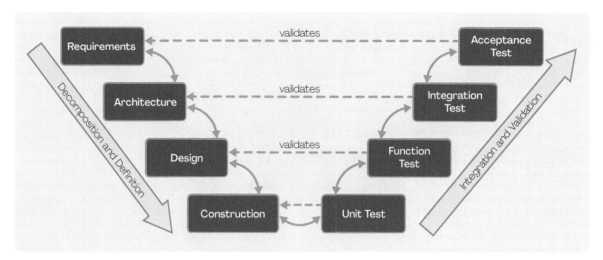

Figure 6.1 The V model for a software development life cycle.

idea is that a team works through functional phases, such as requirements, architecture, and so on. At the end of each phase there is often a "quality gate" milestone review which tends to focus on reviewing documentation. Testing occurs toward the end of the life cycle, and each testing phase, at least in the V model, tends to correspond to an artifact-creation phase earlier in the life cycle. The V model life cycle is based on 1960s/1970s theories about how software development should work. Note that some organizations in the early 1990s and 2000s mistakenly instantiated rational unified process (RUP) as a heavyweight process, so some practitioners think that RUP is a traditional process too. No, RUP is iterative and incremental, but was often implemented poorly by people who didn't move away from the traditional mindset.

If the serial approach is explicitly not currently included in DAD, why are we talking about it? Because some teams are currently following a serial approach and need help moving away from it. Worse yet, there are many people who believe that traditional strategies are applicable to a wide range of situations. In one sense they are correct, but what they don't understand is that agile/lean strategies prove much better in practice for most of those situations. But, as you'll learn later in this chapter, there are a few situations where traditional strategies do in fact make sense. But just a few.

The Project Mindset Leads to Agile Phases, and That's Okay

Many organizations choose to fund solution delivery in terms of projects. These projects may be date-driven and have a defined start and end date, they may be scope-driven in that they must deliver specific functionality or a specific set of outcomes, or they may be cost-driven in that they must come in on or under a desired budget. Some projects have a combination of these constraints, but the more constraints you put on a delivery team, the greater the risk of project failure. Figure 6.2 depicts a high-level view of the project delivery life cycle, and as you see, it has three phases:

1. **Inception.** Inception is sometimes called "sprint 0," "iteration 0," startup, or initiation. The basic idea is that the team does just enough work to get organized and going in the right direction. The team will initially form itself and invest some time in initial requirements and architecture exploration, initial planning, aligning itself with the rest of the organization, and of course,

Agile History Lesson

The term "iteration 0" was first coined by Jim Highsmith, one of the creators of the Agile Manifesto, in his book *Agile Software Development Ecosystems* in 2002 [Highsmith]. It was later adopted and renamed Sprint 0 by the Scrum community.

securing funding for the rest of the project. This phase should be kept as simple and as short as possible while coming to an agreement on how the team believes it will accomplish the outcomes being asked of it by their stakeholders. The average agile/lean team spends 11 work days, so a bit more than 2 weeks, in Inception activities [SoftDev18].

2. **Construction.** The aim of Construction is to produce a consumable solution with sufficient customer value, what's known as a minimum business increment (MBI), to be of value to stakeholders. The team will work closely with stakeholders to understand their needs, to build a quality solution for them, to get feedback from them on a regular basis, and then act on that feedback. The implication is that the team will be performing analysis, design, programming, testing, and management activities potentially every single day. More on this later.

3. **Transition.** Transition is sometimes referred to as a "release sprint" or a "deployment sprint," and if the team is struggling with quality, a "hardening sprint." The aim of Transition is to successfully release your solution into production. This includes determining whether you are ready to deploy the solution and then actually deploying it. The average agile/lean team spends 6 work days on Transition activities, but when you exclude the teams that have fully automated testing and deployment (which we wouldn't do), it's an average of 8.5 days [SoftDev18]. Furthermore, 26% of teams have fully automated regression testing and deployment, and 63% perform Transition in 1 day or less.

Although agile purists will balk at the concept of phases, and will often jump through hoops such as calling Inception "sprint 0" and Transition a "release sprint," the fact is that agile project teams work in a serial manner at a high level. Teams need to invest some time at the beginning to get going in the right direction (Inception/sprint 0), they need to spend time producing the solution (Construction), and they need to spend time deploying the solution (Transition/release sprint). This happens in

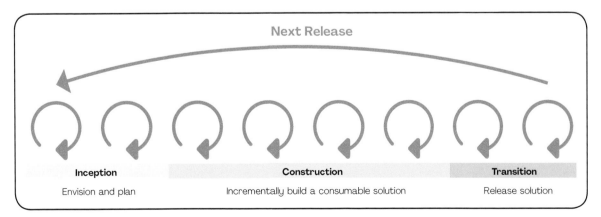

Figure 6.2 The agile project life cycle (high level).

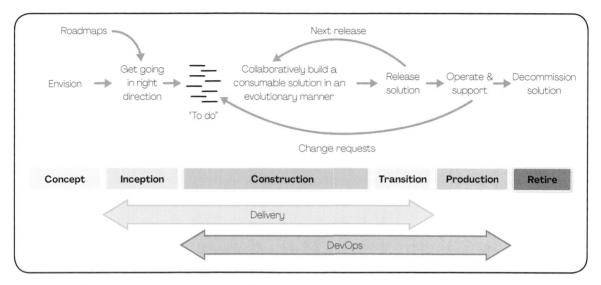

Figure 6.3 The system/solution/product life cycle (high level).

practice and is very easy to observe if you choose to. The important thing is to streamline your Inception and Transition efforts as much as possible, and Construction, too, for that matter.

There is more to IT, and your organization in general, than solution delivery. For example, your organization is likely to have data management, enterprise architecture, operations, portfolio management, marketing, vendor management, finance, and many other important organizational aspects. A full system/product life cycle goes from the initial concept for the solution, through delivery, to operations and support and often includes many rounds through the delivery life cycle. Figure 6.3 depicts the system life cycle, showing how the delivery life cycle, and the DevOps life cycle for that matter, is a subset of it. Although Figure 6.3 adds the Concept (ideation), Production, and Retire phases, the focus of DAD and this book is on delivery. Disciplined Agile (DA), as you learned in Chapter 1, includes strategies that encompass DAD, Disciplined DevOps, value streams, and the Disciplined Agile Enterprise (DAE) in general [DALayers].

Shift Left, Shift Right, Deliver Continuously

Although some teams will take a project-based approach, not all of them do and over time we expect this trend to grow. When a team is allowed to stay together for a long period of time, typically longer than a single project, we call this a stable or long-standing team. When a long-standing team is allowed to evolve its WoW, we've seen some incredible things happen—they become teams capable of continuous delivery. The term "shift left" is popular among agilists, often being used to indicate that testing and quality practices are being performed throughout the entire life cycle. This is a good thing, but there's more to the "shifting" trend than this. There are several important trends, summarized in Figure 6.4, that will affect the way a team evolves its WoW:

1. **Testing and quality practices shift left.** Agilists are clearly shifting testing practices left through greater automation and via replacing written specifications with executable specifications via practices such as test-driven development (TDD) [Beck] and behavior-driven development (BDD) [ExecutableSpecs]. TDD and BDD, of course, are supported by the practice of continuous

integration (CI) [HumbleFarley]. Adoption of these strategies is a key motivator for an infrastructure-as-code strategy where activities that are mostly manual on traditional teams become fully automated on agile teams.

2. **Modeling and planning practices shift right.** Agilists have also shifted modeling/mapping and planning practices to the right in the life cycle so that we can adapt to the feedback we're receiving from stakeholders. In DAD, modeling and planning are so important that we do them all the way through the life cycle in a collaborative and iterative manner [AgileModeling].

3. **Stakeholder interaction shifts right.** DAD teams interact with stakeholders throughout the entire endeavor, not just during the requirements and test phases at the beginning and end of the life cycle.

4. **Stakeholder feedback shifts left.** Traditional teams tend to leave serious stakeholder feedback to user acceptance testing (UAT) performed during the traditional test phase. DAD teams, on the other hand, seek to gain stakeholder feedback as early and as regularly as possible throughout the entire endeavor.

5. **Deployment practices shift left.** Deployment practices are being fully automated by agile teams, another infrastructure-as-code strategy, to support continuous deployment (CD). CD is a linchpin practice for DAD's two continuous delivery life cycles described below.

6. **The real goal is continuous delivery.** All of this shifting left and shifting right results in teams that are able to work in a continuous delivery manner. Process improvement is about working smarter, not harder.

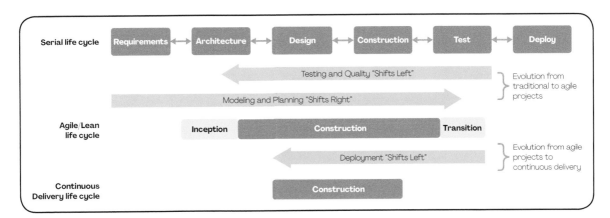

Figure 6.4 How life cycles evolve when you shift activities left and right.

Choice Is Good: DAD's Life Cycles

DAD supports several life cycles for teams to choose from. These life cycles, described in detail below and summarized in Figure 6.5, are:

1. **Agile.** Based on the Scrum construction life cycle, teams following this project life cycle will produce consumable solutions via short iterations (also known as sprints or timeboxes).
2. **Continuous Delivery: Agile.** Teams following this agile-based life cycle will work in very short iterations, typically 1 week or less, where at the end of each iteration their solution is released into production.
3. **Lean.** Based on Kanban, teams following this project life cycle will visualize their work, reduce work in process (WIP) to streamline their workflow, and pull work into the team one item at a time.
4. **Continuous Delivery: Lean.** Teams following this lean-based life cycle will release their work into production whenever possible, typically several times a day.

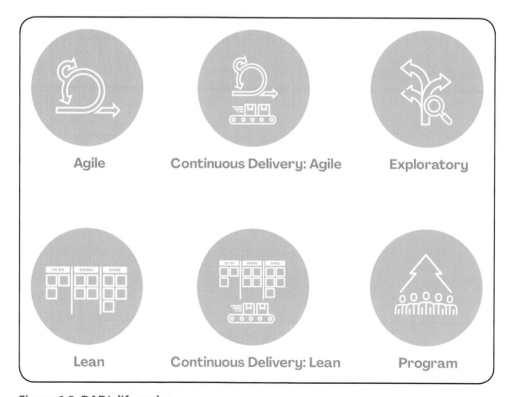

Figure 6.5 DAD's life cycles.

5. **Exploratory.** Teams following this life cycle, based on Lean Startup [Ries] and design thinking in general, will explore a business idea by developing one or more minimum viable products (MVPs), which they run as experiments to determine what potential customers actually want. This life cycle is often applied when a team faces a "wicked problem" [WickedProblemSolving] in their domain.

6. **Program.** A program is effectively a large team that is organized into a team of teams.

Now let's explore each of these life cycles in greater detail. After that, we'll discuss when to consider adopting each one.

DAD's Agile Life Cycle

DAD's agile life cycle, shown in Figure 6.6, is based largely upon the Scrum life cycle with proven governance concepts adopted from the Unified Process (UP) to make it enterprise ready [Kruchten]. This life cycle is often adopted by project teams focused on developing a single release of a solution, although sometimes a team will stay together and follow it again for the next release (and the next release after that, and so on). In many ways, this life cycle depicts how a Scrum-based project life cycle works in an enterprise-class setting. We've worked with several teams that like to think of this as Scrum++, without being constrained by the Scrum community's cultural imperative to gloss over the activities of solution delivery that they find inconvenient. There are several critical aspects to this life cycle:

- **The Inception phase.** As we described earlier, the team's focus is to do just enough work to get organized and going in the right direction. DAD aims to streamline the entire life cycle from beginning to end, including the initiation activities addressed by Inception. Inception ends when we have an agreed-upon vision regarding the expected outcomes for the team and how we're going to achieve them.

- **Construction is organized into short iterations.** An iteration is a short period of time, typically 2 weeks or less, in which the delivery team produces a new, potentially consumable version of their solution. Of course, for a new product or solution you may not have something truly consumable until after having completed several iterations. This phase ends when we have sufficient customer value, also known as a minimum business increment (MBI).

- **Teams address work items in small batches.** Working in small batches is a fundamental of Scrum, and because this life cycle is based on Scrum, it's an important aspect of it. DAD teams, regardless of life cycle, are likely to work on a range of things: implementing new functionality, providing stakeholders with positive outcomes, running experiments, addressing end-user change requests coming in from usage of the current solution running in production, paying down technical debt, taking training, and many more. Work items are typically prioritized by the product owner, primarily by business value although risk, due dates, and severity (in the case of change requests) may also be considered. The Intake Work process goal provides a range of options for managing work items. In each iteration, the team pulls a small batch of work off the work item list that they believe they can achieve during that iteration.

- **Critical ceremonies have a defined cadence.** Like Scrum, this life cycle schedules several agile ceremonies on specific cadences. At the beginning of each iteration, the team performs detailed planning for the iteration, and at the end of the iteration, we hold a demonstration. We hold a retrospective to evolve our WoW, and we make a go-forward decision. We also hold a daily coordination meeting. The point is that by prescribing when to hold these important work sessions, we take some of the guess work out of the process. The downside is that Scrum

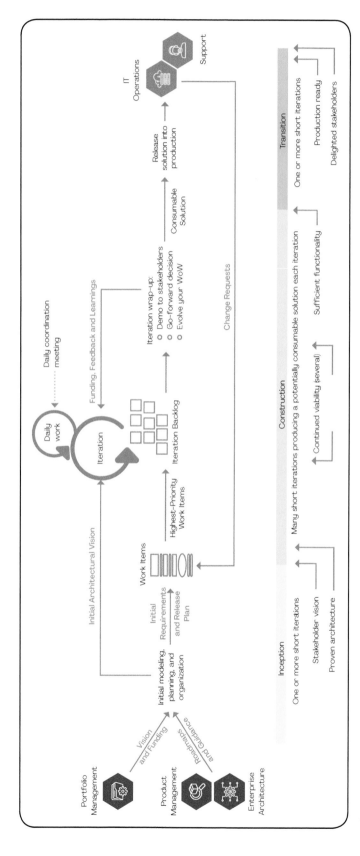

Figure 6.6 DAD's Agile life cycle.

injects a fair bit of process overhead with ceremonies. This is a problem that the Lean life cycle addresses.

- **The Transition phase.** The aim of the Transition phase is to ensure that the solution is ready to be deployed and, if so, to deploy it. This "phase" can be automated away (which is exactly what happens when evolving toward the two continuous delivery life cycles).
- **Explicit milestones.** This life cycle supports the full range of straightforward, risk-based milestones, as you see depicted along the bottom of the life cycle. The milestones enable leadership to govern effectively, more on this later. By "lightweight" we mean that milestones do not need to be a formal bureaucratic review of artifacts. Ideally, they are merely placeholders for discussions regarding the status and health of the initiative.
- **Enterprise guidance and roadmaps are explicitly shown.** On the left-hand side of the life cycle, you see that important flows come into the team from outside of the delivery life cycle. That's because solution delivery is just part of your organization's overall DevOps strategy, which in turn is part of your overall IT strategy. For example, the initial vision and funding for your endeavor may be coming from a product management group, and the roadmaps and guidance from other areas such as enterprise architecture, data management, and security (to name a few). Remember, DAD teams work in an enterprise-aware manner, and one aspect of doing so is to adopt and follow appropriate guidance.
- **Operations and support are depicted.** If your team is working on the new release of an existing solution, then you are likely to receive change requests from existing end users, typically coming to you via your operations and support efforts. For teams working in a DevOps environment, it may be that you're responsible for running and supporting your solution in production.

DAD's Continuous Delivery: Agile Life Cycle

DAD's Continuous Delivery: Agile life cycle, shown in Figure 6.7, is a natural progression from the Agile life cycle of Figure 6.6. Teams typically evolve to this life cycle from the Agile life cycle, often adopting iteration lengths of 1 week or less. The key difference between this and the Agile life cycle is that the Continuous Delivery: Agile life cycle results in a release of new functionality at the end of each iteration rather than after several iterations. There are several critical aspects to this life cycle:

- **Automation and technical practices are key.** Teams require a mature set of technical practices around automated regression testing, continuous integration (CI), and continuous deployment (CD). To support these practices, investment in tools and paying down technical debt, and in particular writing the automated regression tests that are missing, needs to occur.
- **Inception occurred in the past.** When the team was first initiated, Inception would have occurred and it may have occurred again when significant change occurred, such as a major shift in business direction or technical direction. So, if such a shift occurs again then, yes, you should definitely invest sufficient effort to reorient the team. We see this as an activity, not a phase, hence Inception isn't depicted. Having said this, we do see teams stop every few months and explicitly invest several days to negotiate, at a high level, what they will do for the next few months. This is something that SAFe calls big room planning and Agile Modeling calls an agile modeling session. These techniques are discussed in the Coordinate Activities process goal.
- **Transition has become an activity.** Through automation of testing and deployment, the Transition phase has evolved from a multiday or multiweek effort to a fully automated activity that takes minutes or hours.

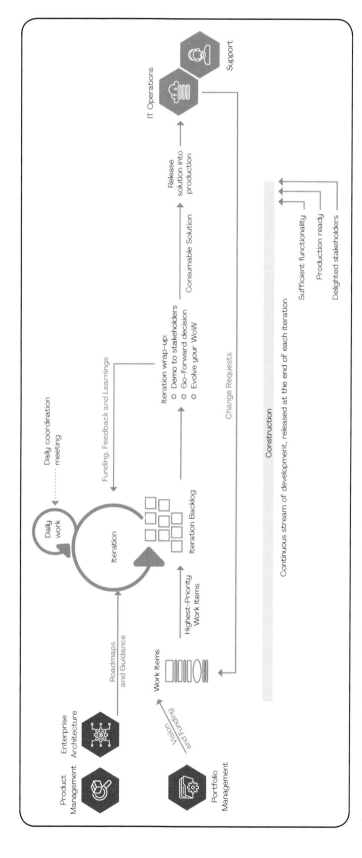

Figure 6.7 DAD's Continuous Delivery: Agile life cycle.

- **Explicit milestones and incoming workflows.** There are still common, risk-based milestones to support consistent governance. Some milestones are no longer appropriate, in particular Stakeholder Vision and Proven Architecture would have been addressed in the past (although if major changes occur, there's no reason why you couldn't address these milestones again). Incoming workflows from other parts of the organization are shown, just as with the Agile and Lean life cycles.

DAD's Lean Life Cycle

DAD's Lean life cycle, shown in Figure 6.8, promotes lean principles, such as minimizing work in process, maximizing flow, a continuous streaming of work (instead of fixed iterations), and reducing bottlenecks. This project-oriented life cycle is often adopted by teams that are new to agile/lean that face rapidly changing stakeholder needs, a common issue for teams evolving (sustaining) an existing legacy solution, and by traditional teams that don't want to take on the risk of the cultural and process disruption usually caused by agile adoption (at least not right away). There are several critical aspects to this life cycle:

- **Teams address work items one at a time.** A major difference between the Lean and Agile life cycles is the lack of iterations. New work is pulled from the work item pool one item at a time as the team has capacity, as opposed to the iteration-based approach where it is pulled into the team in small batches.
- **Work items are prioritized just in time (JIT).** Work items are maintained as a small options pool, often organized into categories by prioritization time—some work items are prioritized by value (and hopefully risk) or a fixed delivery date, some must be expedited (often a severity 1 production problem or request from an important stakeholder), and some work is intangible (such as paying down technical debt or going on training). Prioritization is effectively performed on a JIT basis, with the team choosing the most important work item at the time when they pull it in to be worked on.
- **Practices are performed when needed, as needed.** As with work prioritization, other practices such as planning, holding demos, replenishing the work item pool, holding coordination meetings, making go-forward decisions, look-ahead modeling, and many others are performed on a JIT basis. This tends to remove some of the overhead that teams experience with the Agile life cycle, but requires more discipline to decide when to perform the various practices.
- **Teams actively manage their workflow.** Lean teams use a kanban board [Anderson] to manage their work. A kanban board depicts the team's high-level process in terms of state, with each column on the board representing a state such as Needs a Volunteer, Being Explored, Waiting for Dev, Being Built, Waiting for Test, Being Tested, and Done. Those were just examples, because as teams choose their WoW, every team will develop a board that reflects their WoW. Kanban boards are often implemented on whiteboards or via agile management software. Work is depicted in the form of tickets (stickies on the whiteboard), with a ticket being a work item from the options pool/backlog or a subtask of a work item. Each column has a work-in-progress (WIP) limit that puts an upper limit on the number of tickets that may be in that state. As the team performs their work, they pull the corresponding tickets through the process on their kanban board to coordinate their work.
- **Explicit phases, milestones, and incoming workflows.** There is still an Inception phase and a Transition phase as well risk-based milestones to support consistent governance. Incoming workflows from other parts of the organization are shown, just as with the Agile life cycle.

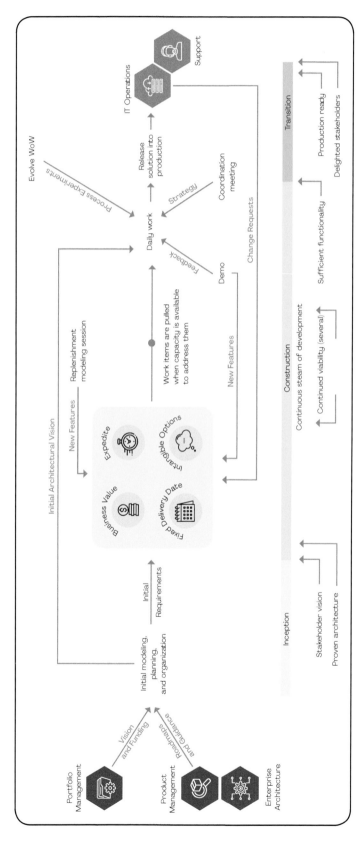

Figure 6.8 DAD's Lean life cycle.

Outcomes Lead to Continuous Exploration

An interesting thing that we've observed is that when you capture work items as outcomes, instead of as requirements such as user stories, this life cycle tends to evolve into continuous exploration of stakeholder needs rather than the continuous order taking that we see with requirements-driven strategies.

DAD's Continuous Delivery: Lean Life Cycle

DAD's Continuous Delivery: Lean life cycle, shown in Figure 6.9, is a natural progression from the Lean life cycle. Teams typically evolve into this life cycle from either the Lean life cycle or the Continuous Delivery: Agile life cycle. There are several critical aspects to this life cycle:

- **Delivery of new functionality is truly continuous.** Changes to production are delivered several times a day by the team, although the functionality may not be turned on until it is needed (this is a DevOps strategy called feature toggles).
- **Automation and technical practices are key.** This is similar to the Continuous Delivery: Agile life cycle.
- **Inception and Transition have disappeared from the diagram.** This occurred for the same reasons they disappeared for the Continuous Delivery: Agile life cycle.
- **Explicit milestones and incoming workflows.** Once again, this is similar to the Continuous Delivery: Agile life cycle.

DAD's Exploratory Life Cycle

DAD's Exploratory life cycle, shown in Figure 6.10, is based on the Lean Startup principles advocated by Eric Ries. The philosophy of Lean Startup is to minimize up-front investments in developing new products/services (offerings) in the marketplace in favor of small experiments [Ries]. The idea is to run some experiments with potential customers to identify what they want based on actual usage, thereby increasing our chance of producing something they're actually interested in. This approach of running customer-facing experiments to explore user needs is an important design thinking strategy for exploring "wicked problems" in your domain. There are several critical aspects to this life cycle:

- **This is a simplified scientific method.** We come up with a hypothesis of what our customers want, we develop one or more minimum viable products (MVPs) which are deployed to a subset of potential customers, then we observe and measure how they work with the MVP(s). Based on the data we collect, we decide how we will go forward. Do we pivot and rethink our hypothesis? Do we rework one or more MVPs to run new experiments based on our improved understanding of customer needs? Do we discard one or more ideas? Do we move forward with one or more ideas and "productize them" into real customer offerings?
- **MVPs are investments in learning.** The MVPs we create are built hastily, often "smoke and mirrors" or prototype-quality code, of which the sole purpose is to test out a hypothesis. It is

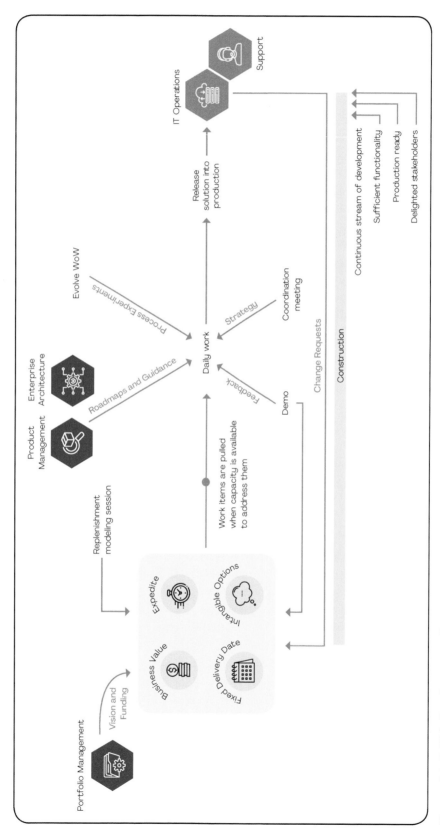

Figure 6.9 DAD's Continuous Delivery: Lean life cycle.

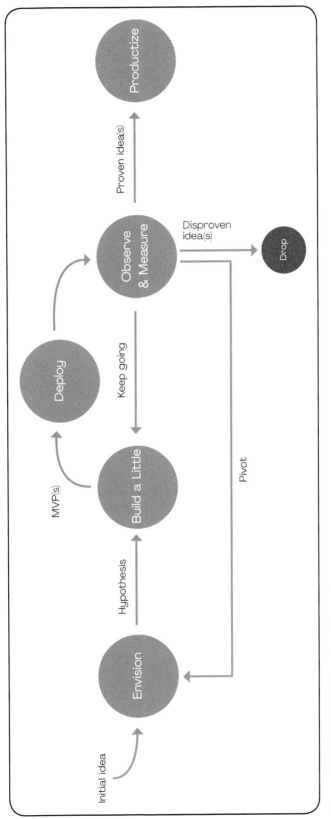

Figure 6.10 DAD's Exploratory life cycle.

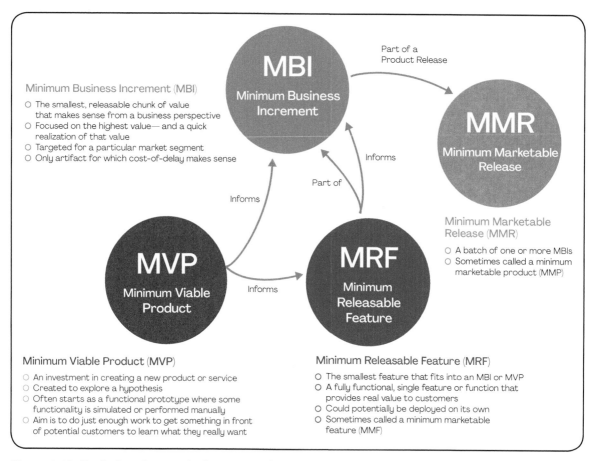

Figure 6.11 Exploring the terminology around MVPs.

not the "real thing," nor is it meant to be. It's a piece of functionality or service offering that we get out in front of our potential customers to see how they react to it. See Figure 6.11 for an overview of MVPs and related concepts.

- **Run several experiments in parallel.** Ideally, this life cycle entails running several experiments in parallel to explore our hypothesis. This is an improvement over Lean Startup, which focuses on a single experiment at a time—although it is easier to run a single experiment at a time, it takes longer to get to a good idea and, worse yet, runs the risk of identifying a strategy before other options have been considered.
- **Failed experiments are still successes.** Some organizations are reluctant to run experiments because they fear failing, which is unfortunate because an exploratory approach such as this actually reduces your risk of product failure (which tend to be large, expensive, and embarrassing). Our advice is to make it "safe to fail," to recognize that when an experiment has a negative result that this is a success because you have inexpensively learned what won't work, enabling you to refocus on looking for something that will.
- **Follow another life cycle to build the real product.** Once we've discovered one or more ideas that it appears will succeed in the market, we now need to build the "real solution." We do this by following one of the other DAD life cycles.

We've seen several different flavors, or perhaps several different tailorings is a better way of looking at it, over the years:

1. **Exploration of a new offering.** The most compelling reason, at least for us, is to apply this life cycle to explore an idea that your organization has for a new product.
2. **Exploration of a new feature.** At a smaller scale, the Exploratory life cycle is effectively the strategy for running an A/B test or split test where you implement several versions of a new feature and run them in parallel to determine which one is most effective.
3. **Parallel proofs of concept (PoC).** With a PoC, you install and then evaluate a package, sometimes called a commercial off-the-shelf solution (COTS), within your environment. An effective way to decrease the risk of software acquisition is to run several proofs of concept in parallel, one for each potential software package that you are considering, and then compare the results to identify the best option available. This is often referred to as a "bake-off."
4. **Strategy comparisons.** Some organizations, particularly ones in very competitive environments, will start up several teams initially to work on a product. Each team basically works through Inception, and perhaps even a bit of Construction, the aim being to identify a vision for the product and prove out their architectural strategy. In this case, their work is more advanced than an MVP but less advanced than an MBI. Then, after a period of time, they compare the work of the teams and pick the best approach—the "winning team" gets to move forward and become the product team.

DAD's Program Life Cycle for a "Team of Teams"

DAD's Program life cycle, shown in Figure 6.12, describes how to organize a team of teams. Large agile teams are rare in practice, but they do happen. This is exactly the situation that scaling frameworks such as SAFe, LeSS, and Nexus address. There are several critical aspects to this life cycle:

*   **There's an explicit Inception phase.** Like it or not, when a team is new, we need to invest some up-front time getting organized, and this is particularly true for large teams given the additional risk we face. We should do so as quickly as possible, and the best way is to explicitly recognize what we need to do and how we'll go about doing so.
*   **Subteams/squads choose and then evolve their WoW.** Subteams, sometimes referred to as squads, should be allowed to choose their own WoW just like any other team would. This includes choosing their own life cycles as well as their own practices—to be clear, some teams may be following the Agile life cycle, some the Continuous Delivery: Lean life cycle, and so on. We may choose to impose some constraints on the teams, such as following common guidance and common strategies around coordinating within the program (captured by the Coordinate Activities process goal). As Figure 6.13 implies, we will need to come to an agreement around how we'll proceed with cross-team system integration and cross-team testing (if needed), options for which are captured by the Accelerate Value Delivery process goal and the Develop Test Strategy process goal, respectively. Where a framework such as SAFe would prescribe a strategy such as a release train to do this, DAD offers choices and helps you to pick the best strategy for your situation.
*   **Subteams can be feature teams or component teams.** For years within the agile community, there has been a debate around feature teams versus component teams. A feature team works vertical slices of functionality, implementing a story or addressing a change request from the

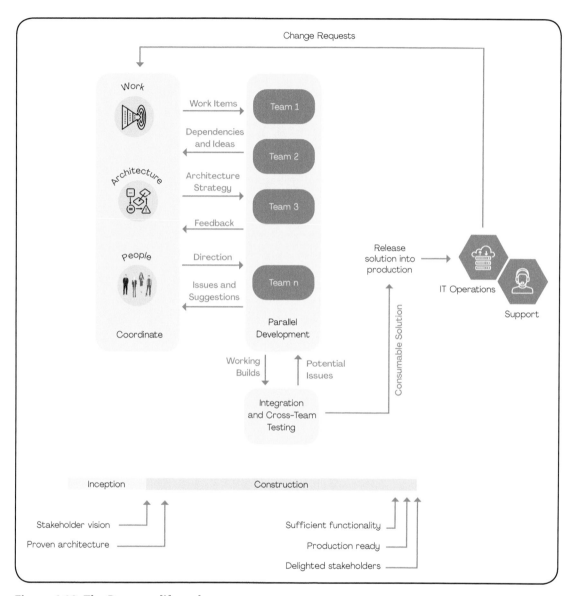

Figure 6.12 The Program life cycle.

user interface all the way through to the database. A component team works on a specific aspect of a system, such as security functionality, transaction processing, or logging. Our experience is both types of teams have their place, they are applicable in certain contexts but not others, and the strategies can and often are combined in practice.

- **Coordination occurs at three levels.** When we're coordinating between subteams, there are three issues we need to be concerned about: coordinating the work to be done, coordinating technical/architectural issues, and coordinating people issues. In Figure 6.13, this coordination is respectively performed by the product owners, the architecture owners, and the team leads. The product owners of each subteam will self-organize and address work/requirements management issues among themselves, ensuring that each team is doing the appropriate work at the appropriate time. Similarly, the architecture ownership team will self-organize to

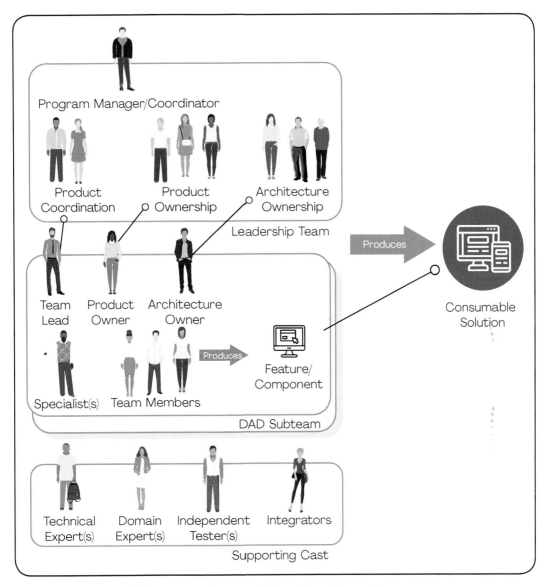

Figure 6.13 A potential structure for organizing a large team of teams.

evolve the architecture over time and the team leads will self-organize to manage people issues occurring across teams. The three leadership subteams are able to handle the type of small course corrections that are typical over time. The team may find that they need to get together occasionally to plan out the next block of work—this is a technique that SAFe refers to as program increment (PI) planning and suggests that it occurs quarterly. We suggest that you do it when and if it makes sense.

- **System integration and testing occurs in parallel.** Figure 6.12 shows that there is a separate team to perform overall system integration and cross-team testing. Ideally, this work should be minimal and entirely automated in time. We frequently need a separate team at first, often due to lack of automation, but our goal should be to automate as much of this work as possible and push the rest into the subteams. Having said that, we've found that usability testing across the whole solution, and similarly user acceptance testing (UAT), requires a separate effort for logistical reasons.

- **Subteams are as whole as they can be.** The majority of the testing effort should occur within the subteams just like it would on a normal agile team, along with continuous integration (CI) and continuous deployment (CD).
- **We can deploy any time we want.** We prefer a CD approach to this, although teams new to agile programs may start by releasing quarterly (or even less often) and then improve the release cadence over time. Teams that are new to this will likely need a Transition phase, some people call these "hardening sprints" or "deployment sprints" the first few times. The Accelerate Value Delivery process goal captures various release options for delivery teams and the Release Management process blade [ReleaseManagement] captures options for the organization level. A process blade encompasses a cohesive collection of process options, such as practices and strategies, that should be chosen and then applied in a context-sensitive manner. Each process blade addresses a specific capability, such as finance, data management, marketing, or vendor management—just like process goals are described using process goal diagrams, so are process blades.
- **Scaling is hard.** Some problems require a large team, but to succeed you need to know what you're doing. If you're struggling with small-team agile, then you're not ready for large-team agile. Furthermore, as we learned in Chapter 3, team size is only one of six scaling factors that our team may need to contend with, the others being geographic distribution, domain complexity, technical complexity, organizational distribution, and regulatory compliance. We cover these issues in greater detail at PMI.org/disciplined-agile/agility-at-scale.

When Should You Adopt Each Life Cycle?

Every team should choose its own life cycle, but how do you do this? It's tempting to have your portfolio management team make this choice—well, at least it is for them. At best, they should make a (hopefully solid) suggestion when they first initiate an endeavor, but in the end the choice of life cycle should be made by the team if you want it to be effective. This can be a challenging choice, particularly for teams new to agile and lean. An important part of the process-decision scaffolding provided by DAD is advice for choosing a life cycle, including the flowchart of Figure 6.14.

Of course, there's a bit more to it than this flowchart. Figure 6.15 overviews what we've found to be important factors, from the Situation Context Framework (SCF) [SCF], to consider when selecting a life cycle. Constraining factors we keep in mind when choosing a delivery life cycle include:

1. **Team skills.** The two continuous delivery (CD) life cycles require the team to have a lot of skill and discipline. The other DAD life cycles also require skill and discipline, although the two CD life cycles stand out. With the serial life cycle, you can get away with lower-skilled people—due to the handoff-oriented nature of serial, you can staff each phase with narrowly skilled specialists. Having said that, we have seen many traditional teams with very skilled people on them.
2. **Team and organization culture.** The Agile and Continuous Delivery life cycles require flexibility within the team and within the parts of the organization that the team interacts with. Lean strategies can be applied in organizations with a varying range of flexibility. Serial can, and often is, applied in very rigid situations.
3. **The nature of the problem.** The Continuous Delivery life cycles work very well when you can build and release in very small increments. The other DAD life cycles work very well in small increments. Serial is really geared for big releases.

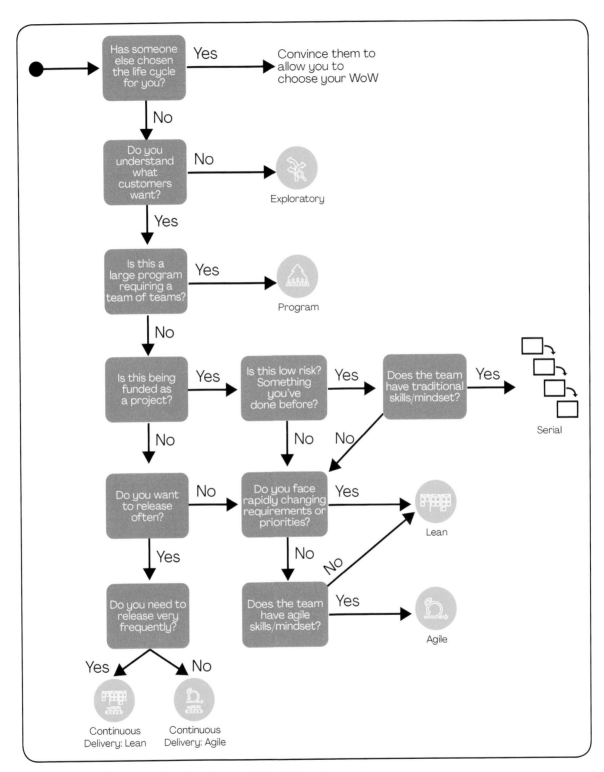

Figure 6.14   A flowchart for choosing an initial life cycle.

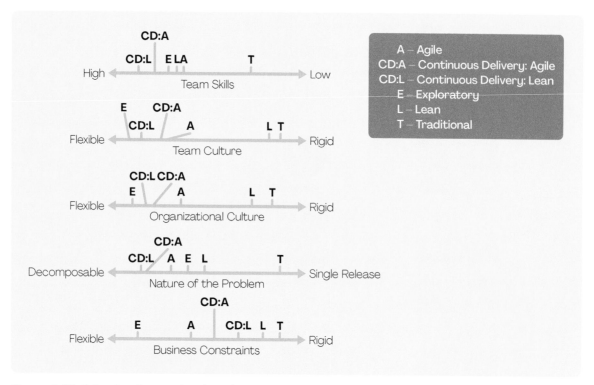

Figure 6.15 Selection factors for choosing a life cycle.

4. **Business constraints.** The key issue here is stakeholder availability and willingness, although financial/funding flexibility is also critical. The Exploratory life cycle requires a flexible, customer-oriented, and experimental mindset on the part of stakeholders. Agile, because it tends to release functionality in terms of complete features, also requires flexibility in the way that we interact with stakeholders. Surprisingly, the Continuous Delivery life cycles require less stakeholder flexibility due to being able to release functionality that is turned off, thereby providing greater control over when something is released (by simply toggling it on).

The Evolve WoW process goal includes a decision point that covers the trade-offs associated with the six DAD life cycles, plus a few others that are not yet explicitly supported by DAD (such as serial).

Different Life Cycles With Common Milestones

In many of the organizations that we've helped to adopt DA, the senior leadership, and often middle management, are very reluctant at first to allow delivery teams to choose their WoW. The challenge is that their traditional mindset often tells them that teams need to follow the same "repeatable process" so that senior leadership may oversee and guide them. There are two significant misconceptions with this mindset: First, we can have common governance across teams without enforcing a common process. A fundamental enabler of this is to adopt common, risk-based (not artifact-based) milestones across the life cycles. This is exactly what DAD does, and these common milestones are shown in Figure 6.16. Second, repeatable outcomes are far more important than repeatable processes. Our stakeholders want us to spend their IT investment wisely. They want us to produce—and evolve—solutions that meet their actual needs. They want these solutions quickly.

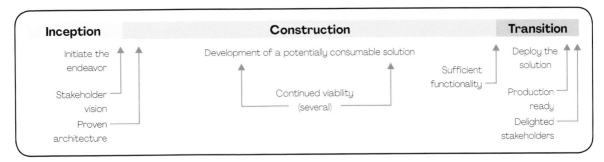

Figure 6.16 Common milestones across the life cycles.

They want solutions that enable them to compete effectively in the marketplace. These are the types of outcomes that stakeholders would like to have over and over (e.g., repeatedly), they really aren't that concerned with the processes that we follow to do this. For more on effective governance strategies for agile/lean teams, see the Govern Team process goal.

Let's explore DAD's risk-based milestones in a bit more detail:

1. **Stakeholder Vision.** The aim of the Inception phase is to spend a short, yet sufficient amount of time, typically a few days to a few weeks, to gain stakeholder agreement that the initiative makes sense and should continue into the Construction phase. By addressing each of the DAD Inception goals, the delivery team will capture traditional project information related to *initial* scope, technology, schedule, budget, risks, and other information, albeit in as simple a fashion as possible. This information is consolidated and presented to stakeholders as a vision statement as described by the Develop Common Vision process goal. The format of the vision and formality of review will vary according to your situation. A typical practice is to review a short set of slides with key stakeholders at the end of the Inception phase to ensure that everyone is on the same page with regard to the project intent and delivery approach.
2. **Proven Architecture.** Early risk mitigation is a part of any good engineering discipline. As the Prove Architecture Early process goal indicates, there are several strategies you may choose

Explicit Phases and Governance Make Agile More Palatable to Management

Daniel Gagnon has been at the forefront of agile practice and delivery for almost a decade in two of Canada's largest financial institutions. He had this to say about using DA as an overarching tool kit: "At both large financials that I have worked in, I set out to demonstrate the pragmatic advantages of using DA as a 'top of the house' approach. Process tailoring in large, complex organizations clearly reveals the need for a large number of context-specific implementations of the four (now five) life cycles, and DA allows for a spectrum of possibilities that no other framework accommodates. However, we call this 'structured freedom' as all choices are still governed by DA's application of Inception, Construction, and Transition with lightweight, risk-based milestones. These phases are familiar to PMOs, which means that we aren't carrying out a frontal assault on their fortified position, but rather introducing governance change in a lean, iterative, and incremental fashion."

to adopt. The most effective of which is to build an end-to-end skeleton of working code that implements technically risky business requirements. A key responsibility of DAD's architecture owner role is to identify risks during the Inception phase. It is expected that these risks will have been reduced or eliminated by implementing related functionality somewhere between one and three iterations into the Construction phase. As a result of applying this approach, early iteration reviews/demos often show the ability of the solution to support nonfunctional requirements in addition to, or instead of, functional requirements. For this reason, it is important that architecture-savvy stakeholders are given the opportunity to participate in these milestone reviews.

3. **Continued Viability.** An optional milestone to include in your release schedule is related to project viability. At certain times during a project, stakeholders may request a checkpoint to ensure that the team is working toward the vision agreed to at the end of Inception. Scheduling these milestones ensures that stakeholders are aware of key dates wherein they should get together with the team to assess the project status and agree to changes if necessary. These changes could include anything such as funding levels, team makeup, scope, risk assessment, or even potentially canceling the project. There could be several of these milestones on a long-running project. However, instead of having this milestone review, the real solution is to release into production more often. Actual usage, or lack thereof, will provide a very clear indication of whether your solution is viable.

4. **Sufficient Functionality.** While it is worthwhile pursuing a goal of a consumable solution (what Scrum calls a potentially shippable increment) at the end of each iteration, it is more common to require a number of iterations of Construction before the team has implemented enough functionality to deploy. While this is sometimes referred to as a minimum viable product (MVP), this not technically accurate as, classically, an MVP is meant to test the viability of a product rather than an indication of minimal deployable functionality. The more accurate term to compare to this milestone would be "minimum feature set" or "minimum business increment" (MBI), as Figure 6.11 shows. An MBI is the smallest viable enhancement to an existing product/service that delivers realized value for a customer. An MBI will comprise one or more minimum marketable features (MMFs), and an MMF provides a positive outcome to the end users of our solution. An outcome may need to be implemented via several user stories. For example, searching for an item on an ecommerce system adds no value to an end user if they cannot also add the found items to their shopping cart. DAD's sufficient functionality milestone is reached at the end of the Construction phase when an MBI is available, plus the cost of transitioning the release to stakeholders is justified. As an example, while an increment of a consumable solution may be available with every 2-week iteration, it may take several weeks to deploy it in a high-compliance environment, so the cost of deployment may not be justified until a greater amount of functionality is completed.

5. **Production Ready.** Once sufficient functionality has been developed and tested, transition-related activities such as data conversions, final acceptance testing, production, and

MVPs Versus MBIs

Daniel Gagnon provides this advice: Think of an MVP as something the organization does for **selfish** reasons. It's all about learning, not about providing the customer with a fully-fledged (or sometimes even vaguely functioning!) solution, whereas an MBI is **altruistic**—it's all about the customer's needs.

support-related documentation normally need to be completed. Ideally, much of the work has been done continuously during the Construction phase as part of completing each increment of functionality. At some point, a decision needs to be made that the solution is ready for production, which is the purpose of this milestone. The two project-based life cycles include a Transition phase where the Production Ready milestone is typically implemented as a review. The two continuous delivery life cycles, on the other hand, have a fully automated transition/release activity where this milestone is addressed programmatically—typically the solution must pass automated regression testing and the automated analysis tools must determine that the solution is of sufficient quality.

6. **Delighted Stakeholders.** Governance bodies and other stakeholders obviously like to know when the initiative is officially over so that they can begin another release or direct funds elsewhere. The initiative doesn't end when the solution is deployed. With projects, there are often closeout activities such as training, deployment tuning, support handoffs, post-implementation reviews, or even warranty periods before the solution is considered complete. One of the principles of DA is to delight customers, which suggests that "satisfied" customers is setting the bar too low. We need to verify whether we've delighted our stakeholders, typically through collection and analysis of appropriate metrics, sometimes called "benefits realization."

Life Cycles Are Just Starting Points

DAD teams will often evolve from one life cycle to another. This is because DAD teams are always striving to Optimize Flow, to improve their WoW as they learn through their experiences and through purposeful experimentation. Figure 6.17 shows common evolution paths that we've seen teams go through. The times indicated in Figure 6.17 reflect our experiences when teams are supported by Disciplined Agile® (DA) training and a Disciplined Agile Coach (DAC)™—without this, expect longer times and most likely higher total costs, on average. When helping a traditional team move to a more effective WoW, a common approach is to start with the Agile life cycle. This is a "sink or swim" approach that experience shows can be very effective, but it can prove difficult in cultures that resist change. A second path shown in this diagram is to start traditional teams with a Lean Kanban [Anderson] approach wherein the team starts with their existing WoW and evolves it over time via small changes into the Lean life cycle. While this is less disruptive, it can result in a much

Life Cycle Evolution Is a Good Thing

To be clear, we think Scrum is great and it is at the heart of our two agile life cycles. However, we have seen a growing backlash in the agile community against its prescriptive aspects. As we describe in our *Introduction to Disciplined Agile Delivery* book, in practice, we regularly see advanced agile/Scrum teams stripping out the process waste in Scrum, such as daily meetings, planning, estimating, and retrospectives as they "lean up." The Scrum community is quick to ostracize such behavior as "Scrum . . . but"—doing some Scrum but not all of it. However, we see this as a natural evolution as the team replaces wasteful activities with added value delivery. The nature of these teams that naturally collaborate all day, every day, means that they don't need to perform such ceremonies on a deferred cadence, preferring to do these things when needed on a JIT basis. We think this is a good and natural thing.

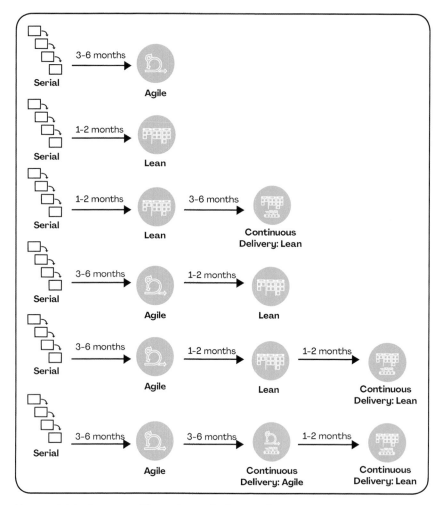

Figure 6.17   Common life cycle evolution paths.

slower rate of improvement since the teams often continue to work in a silo fashion with kanban board columns depicting traditional specialties.

What Figure 6.17 doesn't show is where the Program or Exploratory life cycles fit in. First, in some ways it does apply to the Program life cycle. You can take an agile program approach (similar to what scaling frameworks such as Nexus, SAFe, and LeSS do in practice), where the program releases large increments on a regular cadence (say quarterly). You can also take a lean program approach, where the subteams stream functionality into production and then at the program level this is toggled on when it makes sense to do so. Second, the focus of the diagram is on full-delivery life cycles, whereas the Exploratory life cycle isn't a full-delivery life cycle in its own right. It is typically used to test out a hypothesis regarding a potential marketplace offering, and when the idea has been sufficiently fleshed out and it appears the product will succeed, then the team shifts into one of the delivery life cycles of Figure 6.17. In that way, it replaces a good portion of the Inception phase efforts for the team. Another common scenario is that a team is in the middle of development and realizes that they have a new idea for a major feature that needs to be better explored before investing serious development effort into it. So the team will shift into the Exploratory life cycle for as long as it takes to either flesh out the feature idea or disprove its market viability.

In Summary

In this chapter, we explored several key concepts:

- Some teams within your organization will still follow a serial life cycle—DAD explicitly recognizes this but does not provide support for this shrinking category of work.
- DAD provides the scaffolding required for choosing between, and then evolving, six solution delivery life cycles (SDLCs) based on either agile or lean strategies.
- Project-based life cycles, even agile and lean ones, go through phases.
- Every life cycle has its advantages and disadvantages; each team needs to pick the one that best reflects their context.
- Common, risk-based milestones enable consistent governance—you don't need to force the same process on all of your teams to be able to govern them.
- A team will start with a given life cycle and often evolve away from it as they continuously improve their WoW.

Chapter 7

Disciplined Success

Some people have called Disciplined Agile Delivery (DAD) "complicated" because it focuses on helping you to choose a fit-for-purpose way of working (WoW), rather than simply telling you a small collection of "best practices" that you need to follow. This is unfortunate, as the inconvenient truth is that effective delivery of IT solutions has never been simple and never will be. The Disciplined Agile (DA) tool kit simply holds up a mirror to the inherent complexity that we face as professionals in enterprise-class settings, and gives you the tools to navigate that complexity.

If You Are Doing Agile, You Are Already Using DA

For example, consider Scrum. Scrum is a subset of two of DAD's life cycles. So if you are just doing Scrum, you are essentially doing a form of DAD. However, if Scrum is all that you are referencing, you are likely not aware of some things you should be thinking about, or not using some supplemental practices to help you be most effective. In our experience, if you are struggling to be effective with agile, it may be that you are either unaware of strategies to help you or you are being given advice by inexperienced, unknowledgeable, or purist agile coaches.

DA Is Agile for the Enterprise

Unfortunately, our industry is full of "thought leaders" that believe that their way, often because it is all that they understand, is the one true way. DA is based upon empirical observations from a vast array of industries, organizations, and all types of initiatives, both project and product based, large and small. DA's inherent flexibility and adaptability is one of the reasons it is such a useful tool kit. DA *just makes sense* because it favors:

1. Pragmatic and agnostic *over* purist approaches;
2. Context-driven decisions *over* one-size-fits-all approaches; and
3. Choice of strategies *over* prescriptive approaches.

If you are a "Scrum shop," you very likely are missing some great opportunities to optimize your way of working. Scrum is actually a phenomenally bad life cycle to use in many situations, which is why your organization has teams taking a Lean/Kanban-based approach, or another non-Scrum approach, even as you read this. If you rely solely on Scrum, or a Scrum-based scaling framework such as SAFe, Nexus, or LeSS, we recommend you expand your horizons with DA to expose more suitable approaches and practices.

Learn Faster to Succeed Earlier

Agile is fond of the phrase "fail fast," meaning that the quicker we fail and learn from our mistakes, the quicker we get to what we need. Our experience is that by referencing proven context-based strategies, we fail less and succeed earlier. In our daily work we are continually making decisions, which is why we call DA a process-decision tool kit. Without referencing the tool kit to help with decision-making, sometimes we either forget things we need to consider, or make poor decisions regarding which techniques to experiment with so as to improve our WoW. DA surfaces decision points for discussion, making the implicit, explicit. For instance, when beginning an initiative in Inception and referring to the "Develop Test Strategy" goal diagram, it is like a coach tapping you on the shoulder and asking: "How will we test this thing?"; "What environments do we need?"; "Where will we get the data?"; "What tools?"; "How much is automated versus manual?"; and "Do we test first or test after?" By surfacing these critical decisions for explicit consideration by your team, we reduce the risk of forgetting things, and increase your chance of choosing a strategy that works well for you. We call this guided continuous improvement (GCI).

Use the DA Browser

We've published the goal diagrams at PMI.org/disciplined-agile/process/introduction-to-dad/process-goals so that you have a quick reference. If you want to access the details behind the goal diagrams, they are online at PMI.org/disciplined-agile/da-browser. In practice, we regularly reference goal diagrams in our coaching to point out why certain practices are less effective than others in certain situations, and what alternatives we should consider. Take your favorite device to your retrospectives, and if your team is struggling with effectively meeting a process goal, review which options and tools you can experiment with to remedy the situation. If you are a coach, DA should make you more effective with helping teams to understand the choices and trade-offs they have available to them.

Invest in Certification to Retain Your New Knowledge

We are sure that you have learned about new techniques in this book that will make you a better agile practitioner, increasing your chances of success on your initiatives. The key is to not let these new ideas fade from memory. We encourage you to cement this new knowledge by studying the content to prepare and take the certification tests. The tests are difficult, but passing them results in a worthwhile and credible certification truly worthy of updating your LinkedIn profile. Companies we have worked with have observed that their teams that have made the investment in learning and certification make better decisions and are thus more effective than teams that don't understand their options and trade-offs. Better decisions lead to better outcomes.

Make the investment in learning this material and proving it through certification. You will be a better agilist, and those around you will notice. You can learn more about the PMI® Agile Certification Journey at PMI.org/certifications/agile-certifications.

Please Get Involved

We also suggest that you participate in the Disciplined Agile community. New ideas and practices emerge from the community and are continually incorporated into DA. Let's learn from each other as we all seek to continue to learn and master our craft.

References

[AgileDocumentation] *Agile/Lean Documentation: Strategies for Agile Software Development*. AgileModeling.com/essays/agileDocumentation.htm

[AgileModeling] Agile Modeling Home Page. AgileModeling.com

[AmblerLines2012] *Disciplined Agile Delivery: A Practitioner's Guide to Agile Software Delivery in the Enterprise*. Scott Ambler & Mark Lines, 2012, IBM Press.

[AmblerLines2017] *An Executive's Guide to Disciplined Agile: Winning the Race to Business Agility*. Scott Ambler & Mark Lines, 2017, Disciplined Agile Consortium.

[Anderson] *Kanban: Successful Evolutionary Change for Your Technology Business*. David J. Anderson, 2010, Blue Hole Press.

[Beck] *Extreme Programming Explained: Embrace Change (2nd Edition)*. Kent Beck & Cynthia Andres, 2004, Addison-Wesley Publishing.

[Brooks] *The Mythical Man-Month, 25th Anniversary Edition*. Frederick P. Brooks Jr., 1995, Addison-Wesley.

[CMMI] *The Disciplined Agile Framework: A Pragmatic Approach to Agile Maturity*. DisciplinedAgileConsortium.org/resources/Whitepapers/DA-CMMI-Crosstalk-201607.pdf

[CockburnHeart] Heart of Agile Home Page. HeartOfAgile.com

[CoE] Centers of Excellence (CoE). PMI.org/disciplined-agile/people/centers-of-excellence

[ContinuousImprovement] Continuous Improvement. PMI.org/disciplined-agile/process/continuous-improvement

[CoP] Communities of Practice (CoPs). PMI.org/disciplined-agile/people/communities-of-practice

[Coram] *Boyd: The Fighter Pilot Who Changed the Art of War*. Robert Coram, 2004, Back Bay Books.

[Cynefin] *A Leader's Framework for Decision Making*. David J. Snowden & Mary E. Boone, *Harvard Business Review*, November 2007. hbr.org/2007/11/a-leaders-framework-for-decision-making

[DABrowser] The Disciplined Agile Browser. PMI.org/disciplined-agile/da-browser

[DADRoles] Roles on DAD Teams. PMI.org/disciplined-agile/people/roles-on-dad-teams

[DAHome] Disciplined Agile Home Page. PMI.org/disciplined-agile

[DALayers] Layers of the Disciplined Agile Tool Kit. PMI.org/disciplined-agile/ip-architecture/layers-of-the-disciplined-agile-tool-kit

[Deming] *The New Economics for Industry, Government, Education*. W. Edwards Deming, 2002, MIT Press.

[Denning] *The Agile of Agile: How Smart Companies Are Transforming the Way Work Gets Done*. Stephen Denning, 2018, AMACON.

[Doer] *Measure What Matters: How Google, Bono, and the Gates Foundation Rock the World with OKRs*. John Doer, 2018, Penguin Publishing Group.

[DSDM] *Dynamic Systems Development Method (DSDM)*. Jennifer Stapleton, 1997, Addison-Wesley Professional.

[ExecutableSpecs] *Specification by Example: How Successful Teams Deliver the Right Software*. Gojko Adzic, 2011, Manning Press.

[Fowler] *The State of Agile Software in 2018*. Martin Fowler, MartinFowler.com/articles/agile-aus-2018.html

[Gagnon] *A Retrospective on Years of Process Tailoring Workshops*. Daniel Gagnon, 2018, ProjectManagement.com/blog-post/61957/A-retrospective-on-years-of-process-tailoring-workshops

[GenSpec] *Generalizing Specialists: Improving Your IT Career Skills*. AgileModeling.com/essays/generalizingSpecialists.htm

[Goals] Process Goals. PMI.org/disciplined-agile/process-goals

[Goldratt] *The Goal: A Process of Ongoing Improvement—3rd Revised Edition*. Eli Goldratt, 2004, North River Press.

[Google] *Five Keys to a Successful Google Team*. Julia Rozovsky, n.d., https://rework.withgoogle.com/blog/five-keys-to-a-successful-google-team/

[GQM] *The Goal Question Metric Approach*. Victor R. Basili, Gianluigi Caldiera, & H. Dieter Rombach,1994, http://www.cs.toronto.edu/~sme/CSC444F/handouts/GQM-paper.pdf

[Highsmith] *Agile Software Development Ecosystems*. Jim Highsmith, 2002, Addison-Wesley.

[Host] The Host Leadership Community. HostLeadership.com

[HumbleFarley] *Continuous Delivery: Reliable Software Releases through Build, Test, and Deployment Automation*. Jez Humble & David Farley, 2010, Addison-Wesley Professional.

[Kim]. *DevOps Cookbook*. RealGeneKim.me/devops-cookbook/

[Kerievsky] *Modern Agile*. ModernAgile.org/

[Kersten] *Project to Product: How to Survive and Thrive in the Age of Digital Disruption With the Flow Framework*. Mik Kersten, 2018, IT Revolution Press.

[Kerth] *Project Retrospectives: A Handbook for Team Reviews*. Norm Kerth, 2001, Dorset House.

[Kotter] *Accelerate: Building Strategic Agility for a Faster Moving World*. John P. Kotter, 2014, Harvard Business Review Press.

[Kruchten] *The Rational Unified Process: An Introduction 3rd Edition*. Philippe Kruchten, 2003, Addison-Wesley Professional.

[LeanChange1] *The Lean Change Method: Managing Agile Organizational Transformation Using Kanban, Kotter, and Lean Startup Thinking*. Jeff Anderson, 2013, Createspace.

[LeanChange2] Lean Change Management Home Page. LeanChange.org

[LeSS] *The LeSS Framework*. LeSS.works.

[LifeCycles] Full Agile Delivery Life Cycles. PMI.org/disciplined-agile/lifecycle

[Liker] *The Toyota Way: 14 Management Principles from the World's Greatest Manufacturer*. Jeffery K. Liker, 2004, McGraw-Hill.

[LinesAmbler2018] *Introduction to Disciplined Agile Delivery 2nd Edition: A Small Agile Team's Journey from Scrum to Disciplined DevOps*. Mark Lines & Scott Ambler, 2018, Project Management Institute.

[Manifesto] *The Agile Manifesto*. AgileManifesto.org

[MCSF] *Team of Teams: New Rules of Engagement for a Complex World*. S. McChrystal, T. Collins, D. Silverman, & C. Fussel, 2015, Portfolio.

[Meadows] *Thinking in Systems: A Primer*. Daniella H. Meadows, 2015, Chelsea Green Publishing.

[Nonaka] *Toward Middle-Up-Down Management: Accelerating Information Creation*. Ikujiro Nonaka, 1988, https://sloanreview.mit.edu/article/toward-middleupdown-management-accelerating-information-creation/

[Nexus] *The Nexus Guide*. Scrum.org/resources/nexus-guide

[Pink] *Drive: The Surprising Truth About What Motivates Us*. Daniel H. Pink, 2011, Riverhead Books.

[Poppendieck] *The Lean Mindset: Ask the Right Questions*. Mary Poppendieck & Tom Poppendieck, 2013, Addison-Wesley Professional.

[Powers] *Powers' Definition of the Agile Mindset*. AdventuresWithAgile.com/consultancy/powers-definition-agile-mind-set/

[Prison] Tear Down the Method Prisons! Set Free the Practices! I. Jacobson & R. Stimson, *ACM Queue*, January/February 2019.

[Reifer] *Quantitative Analysis of Agile Methods Study (2017): Twelve Major Findings*. Donald J. Reifer, 2017, InfoQ.com/articles/reifer-agile-study-2017

[Reinertsen] *The Principles of Product Development Flow: Second Generation Lean Product Development*. Donald G. Reinertsen, 2012, Celeritis Publishing.

[ReleaseManagement] Release Management. PMI.org/disciplined-agile/process/release-management

[Ries] *The Lean Startup: How Today's Entrepreneurs Use Continuous Innovation to Create Radically Successful Businesses*. Eric Ries, 2011, Crown Business.

[RightsResponsibilities] Team Member Rights and Responsibilities. PMI.org/disciplined-agile/people/rights-and-responsibilities

[Rubin] *Essential Scrum: A Practical Guide to the Most Popular Process*. Ken Rubin, 2012, Addison-Wesley Professional.

[SAFe] *SAFe 4.5 Distilled: Applying the Scaled Agile Framework for Lean Enterprises (2nd Edition)*. Richard Knaster & Dean Leffingwell, 2018, Addison-Wesley Professional.

[SCF] *Scaling Agile: The Situation Context Framework*. PMI.org/disciplined-agile/agility-at-scale/tactical-agility-at-scale/scaling-factors

[SchwaberBeedle] *Agile Software Development With SCRUM*. Ken Schwaber & Mike Beedle, 2001, Pearson.

[Schwartz] *The Art of Business Value*. Mark Schwartz, 2016, IT Revolution Press.

[ScrumGuide] *The Scrum Guide*. Jeff Sutherland & Ken Schwaber, 2018, Scrum.org/resources/scrum-guide

[SenseRespond] *Sense & Respond: How Successful Organizations Listen to Customers and Create New Products Continuously*. Jeff Gothelf & Josh Seiden, 2017, Harvard Business Review Press.

[Sheridan] *Joy, Inc.: How We Built a Workplace People Love*. Richard Sheridan, 2014, Portfolio Publishing.

[SoftDev18] *2018 Software Development Survey Results*. Ambysoft.com/surveys/softwareDevelopment2018.html

[Sutherland] *Scrum: The Art of Doing Twice the Work in Half the Time*. Jeff Sutherland & J. J. Sutherland, 2014, Currency.

[Tailoring] Process Tailoring Workshops. PMI.org/disciplined-agile/process/process-tailoring-workshops

[TDD] *Introduction to Test-Driven Development (TDD)*. Scott Ambler, 2004, AgileData.org/essays/tdd.html

[WomackJones] *Lean Thinking: Banish Waste and Create Wealth in Your Corporation*. James P. Womack & Daniel T. Jones, 1996, Simon & Schuster.

[WickedProblemSolving] Wicked Problem Solving. PMI.org/wicked-problem-solving

Acronyms and Abbreviations

AIC	Agile industrial complex
AINO	Agile in name only
AO	Architecture owner
ATDD	Acceptance test-driven development
BA	Business analyst
BDD	Behavior-driven development
CAS	Complex adaptive system
CCB	Change control board
CD	Continuous deployment
CI	Continuous integration or continuous improvement
CMMI	Capability Maturity Model Integration
CoE	Center of expertise/excellence
CoP	Community of practice
COTS	Commercial off the shelf
DA	Disciplined Agile
DAE	Disciplined Agile Enterprise
DBA	Database administrator
DevOps	Development-Operations
DoD	Definition of done
DoR	Definition of ready
EA	Enterprise architect or enterprise architecture
FT	Functional testing
GCI	Guided continuous improvement
GQM	Goal question metric
ISO	International Organization for Standardization
IT	Information technology
ITIL	Information Technology Infrastructure Library
JIT	Just in time
KPI	Key performance indicator
LeSS	Large Scale Scrum
MBI	Minimum business increment
MMF	Minimum marketable feature
MMP	Minimum marketable product
MMR	Minimum marketable release
MVC	Minimal viable change
MVP	Minimum viable product
OKR	Objectives and key results
OODA	Observe-orient-decide-act
PDCA	Plan-do-check-act
PDSA	Plan-do-study-act
PI	Program increment
PM	Project manager
PMI	Project Management Institute
PMO	Project management office

PO	Product owner
PoC	Proof of concept
ROI	Return on investment
RUP	Rational Unified Process
SAFe	Scaled Agile Framework
SCF	Situation Context Framework
SDLC	System/software/solution delivery life cycle
SLA	Service-level agreement
SME	Subject matter expert
TDD	Test-driven development
ToC	Theory of constraints
UAT	User acceptance test(ing)
UI	User interface
UP	Unified process
WIP	Work in process
XP	Extreme Programming

Index

About the Authors

Scott W. Ambler is the vice president and chief scientist for Disciplined Agile at Project Management Institute where he leads the evolution of the DA tool kit. Scott is the cocreator, along with Mark Lines, of the Disciplined Agile (DA) tool kit and founder of the *Agile Modeling (AM), Agile Data (AD)*, and *Enterprise Unified Process (EUP)* methodologies. He is the co-author of several books, including *Disciplined Agile Delivery, Refactoring Databases, Agile Modeling, Agile Database Techniques, The Object Primer – Third Edition*, and many others. Scott is a frequent keynote speaker at conferences, he blogs at ProjectManagement.com, and you can follow him on Twitter via @scottwambler.

Mark Lines is the vice president for Disciplined Agile at Project Management Institute and a Disciplined Agile Fellow. He is the cocreator of the DA tool kit and is a co-author with Scott Ambler of several books on Disciplined Agile. Mark is a frequent keynote speaker at conferences and you can follow him on Twitter via @mark_lines.